VIRTUOUS INTENTIONS

American Academy of Religion Academy Series

edited by
Susan Thistlethwaite

Number 66
VIRTUOUS INTENTIONS
The Religious Dimension of Narrative

by
Mark Ledbetter

Mark Ledbetter

VIRTUOUS INTENTIONS
The Religious Dimension of Narrative

Scholars Press
Atlanta, Georgia

VIRTUOUS INTENTIONS
The Religious Dimension of Narrative

by
Mark Ledbetter

© 1989
The American Academy of Religion

Library of Congress Cataloging in Publication Data

Ledbetter, Mark.
    Virtuous intentions : the religious dimension of narrative / Mark Ledbetter.
        p.   cm. -- (American Academy of Religion academy series ; no. 66)
    ISBN 1-55540-394-8 (alk. paper). -- ISBN 1-55540-395-6 (pbk. : alk. paper)
    1. American fiction--20th century--History and criticism.
2. Religion and literature--History--20th century. 3. Narration
(Rhetoric)--Religious aspects. 4. Fiction--Religious aspects.
I. Title. II. Series
PS374.R47L44 1989
813'.5209382--dc20   89-38392
                                            CIP

Printed in the United States of America
on acid-free paper

To Margaret

ACKNOWLEDGEMENTS

It is indeed good fortune to be advised well, and I have been fortunate. For the best of counsel I thank David Hesla, Robert Detweiler, and Don Saliers. And for dear friends like Trent Foley, Robert Scott, and Wesley Wachob, who lovingly and dutifully listened when they had heard it all before, I am grateful. Finally, I wish to thank Wesleyan College for an environment that encourages ideas and the Florre Jo and Charles L. Davidson, Sr. Foundation, Inc. for financial assistance in preparing this book.

T. M. L.
Wesleyan College
July 1989

TABLE OF CONTENTS

INTRODUCTION

This study is about the religious nature of narrative, and my central contention is that narrative serves a religious function, namely, the discovery of virtue. In the following pages, I defend a number of important assertions concerning narrative's religious function. The most important of these are: (1) desire is a critical component for the motivation of narrative fiction; (2) narrative technique is not a pattern of discovery; rather, narrative technique is discovery; (3) narrative is an encounter with "otherness," which gives narrative its religious dimension; (4) this contact with otherness reveals a particular virtue as central to a particular narrative, a virtue that establishes a religious world-view within the narrative structure.

In chapter 1, I examine the nature of narrative as desire and demonstrate how the structure of narrative is an act of religious discovery. Most important, I explore how narrative creates a hypothetical world of otherness, a world that has a religious dimension.[1] Drawing upon Mark Schorer's work, I address the all-important idea, particularly for this work, that narrative technique itself is an act of discovery. Narrative is no *a priori* construct, but is itself a process not only revealing hidden meanings but also establishing meaning within and by its very structure.

My work focuses on narrative elements, why and how these elements are religious. The elements of narrative I address are plot, tone, atmosphere, and character.[2] Each has a religious function and dimension unique to itself, yet I emphasize the narrative element of character. I believe, with Henry James, that character is the most critical element of narrative fiction, and more specifically, that one must address the narrative element of character to talk about the religious dimensions of the novel.

My claim that narrative is an act of desire that leads to a revealing of a religious virtue is an extension of my argument that character is the most important element of narrative fiction. Narrative is life-like. The narrative structure of human existence is consistently one religious decision after another, and narrative fiction is no different. Life's narrative structure, as well as fiction's narrative structure, leads to and reveals religious and ethical decision-making that establishes dominant virtues for productive religious or ethical existence. I focus on the narrative element character because I believe that it is the religious link between lived narrative and narrative fiction. Furthermore, the narrative element character, in fiction, is the most demonstrable of narrative's "life-likeness." I do not suggest that character is an autonomous element in narrative and that it alone gives a complete reading of the text. I spend some time demonstrating each element's importance in the narrative, and particularly each element's religious function in the text. The element of character depends on the other elements, plot, tone and atmosphere, to lend substance and quality to the ways we are to understand its place in the fiction.

Chapter 1 concludes by suggesting that the whole narrative process establishes a religious world view. Narrative fiction creates a hypothetical world that possesses a religious or ethical ethos. Each narrative fiction differs, particularly in nuance, in its religious world-view. I discuss what I believe to be three fairly dominant religious world views in Western thought: relational, transcendent, tragic. These world views are dominant in the fiction I address.[3]

Chapters 2, 3, and 4 put theoretical claims into practice. I take three authors, James Agee, Walker Percy, and Robert Penn Warren, and using a prominent novel from each, demonstrate the religious virtue each author establishes, the manner in which it is revealed through the element of character, how one other narrative element plays an important but secondary role in the understanding of character, and how each author, in his discovery of virtue, establishes a religious world view that he believes best informs human existence. I couple a prominent theologian with each author's work to give theological foundation for his particular world-view.

Chapter 5, the concluding chapter, addresses the critical implications obvious throughout my work. I maintain that a critic can do value-oriented literary criticism, avoid imposing moral platitudes on the text, and maintain both the text's and critic's literary integrity. My critical presuppositions in this chapter are that narrative is life-like and that narrative-making is an extension of constructs of lived narrative to fiction and therefore that all narrative is deeply rooted in human existence. Most important, I address the idea that literature has meaning, a very important issue in the post-modern world. The concluding remarks of this chapter suggest a limited yet helpful prolegomenon to a critical theory that allows the post-modern critic to remain true to a hermeneutics of suspicion when addressing a text while at the same time seeking a hermeneutics of restoration. I am confident that literary critics can ask the text questions of meaning and utility without destroying or perverting the text's autonomy with superficial or moralistic readings.

CHAPTER 1

NARRATIVE TECHNIQUE AND RELIGIOUS DISCOVERY

Having established the general direction of this work in my introductory remarks, a specific thesis is now in order. Narrative has religious meaning and function, and is motivated by desire, in particular a desire for an ordered and coherent world. Narrative technique is the process of discovering ordered existence or of dealing with the frustration of the inability to order existence. Narrative technique and structure portray the text's understanding of otherness, a world hypothetical and profound, a world that posits "answers to existential crises," and is therefore religious. One discovers the religious function of narrative by close examination of narrative elements, the most important of which is character. The narrative element of character always involves religious decision-making which establishes a dominant virtue in the narrative fiction. The virtue reveals the text's religious world-view and allows for a value-oriented reading of the text.

A final but important note before proceeding, I wish to suggest a definition of religion that allows me to examine literature--narrative--in this way. I am indebted to Mircea Eliade for my "working definition" of religion. Eliade says that "religion is the paradigmatic solution for every existential crisis."[1] Because the solution is paradigmatic, narrative reveals a virtue or virtues to which a character or characters can turn to again and again to give meaning to his/her existence. The solution itself embodies "otherness," which is the desire that motivates narrative. If the existential crisis is one thing, its solution is an other. Eliade suggests that the solution is religious because contact with an "other" enables a person "to transcend personal situations and finally gain access to the world of spirit."[2] In the case of narrative, character may not gain "the world of spirit," but character often "transcends personal situations." Narrative has a religious function because it not only reveals an "existential crisis," but also because it suggests a "paradigmatic solution" to the crisis. The novels I discuss portray characters who experience particular crises and characters who seek and discover particular solutions to their crises. The completion of the crisis-solution dialectic is narrative's religious function.

I

Narrative fiction is motivated by a desire for an ordered and coherent world-view. The very structure of narrative suggests completion, fullness, and wholeness. Stephen Crites tells us that narrative is "the . . . culture's form capable of expressing coherence."[3] A character is often described according to the meaning or lack of meaning his/her life possesses. The plot of a text suggests planned action somehow informed by a possible and particular end. Setting and atmosphere in a text represent order imposed on character and plot. Tone makes us hopeful or expectant, dejected or frustrated; tone has some prescient notion that completion is imminent.

Yet, this coherent world-view is not merely a reflection of the world "outside" narrative fiction. I am not advocating the "realism" of a Henry James or the Aristotelian notion of mimesis. Somehow fiction will always fall short of and at the same time do more than reflect the world, an idea of which Aristotle was all too aware. Things expressed will always exhibit a certain remoteness from the medium of expression. A gap will always remain between art and life; nonetheless, as Richard Weiman explains, "Fiction is vitally concerned with challenging this gap."[4] Yet the desires that motivate formation of character, tone, and atmosphere, the basic narrative elements of the text, are those same desires, psychological and physical, that are so much a part of the world in which we live.

Narrative is motivated by a desire for meaning, not truth. Meaningful existence orders one's world with a pattern of endurance. It would be naive to say that narrative fiction creates an ordered environment that can easily be imposed on human existence and, in turn, order and give meaning to life. Such a view suggests that narrative is an empirical science and deals explicitly with truth. Frank Kermode points out that narrative is not in the business of truth, but rather meaning.

> All modern interpretation that is not merely an attempt at "recognition" involves some effort to divorce meaning and truth. Some such position is the starting point of all modern hermeneutics except those which are consciously reactionary. The pleasures of interpretation are henceforth limited to loss and disappointment, so that most of us will find the task too hard, or simply

repugnant; and then, abandoning meaning, we slip back
into transparency, the single sense, the truth.[5]

The religious desire that motivates narrative fiction is a wish for
something "other than" what exists at the beginning moment of the
fictive act. Literature "arouses desire" and suggests a way of "dealing
with it."[6] The fulfillment of desire is otherness. It is the idea of
otherness that gives literature its religious nature. Fiction, in most
cases, establishes existential crises and proceeds to suggest something
other than the crises as solutions. The attempt to create "ordered time,"
says Kort, is traditionally a religious act.[7] The attempt to order time is
an attempt to discover something other than the current crises.
Otherness need not be a transcendent, in the sense described by Rudolf
Otto or Giles Gunn, though it can be.[8] Otherness in narrative, needs
only to be the solution other than all other solutions that solves the
crisis established and portrayed by the narrative itself.

I am convinced that the otherness that motivates narrative is
revealed in a single virtue that dominates all other virtues in a particular
fiction. The virtue is revealed by being the most probable solution to
the imminent crisis found in the novel. The virtue may be faith in a
transcendent God that gives hope and expectation in a world hopeless
and chaotic. Perhaps the virtue is *philia*, belief in friends and family,
the possibility of the good life through community and human
relationship. The virtue may be courage. Convinced that the world is
tragic, void of meaning and lacking in purpose, one possesses the
courage to endure the world's worst twists and turns which are beyond
human control and therefore discover a certain nobility in the human
creature's perseverance.

Narrative's desire for end, completion, and coherence is well
demonstrated in Frank Kermode's book, *The Sense of an Ending*.[9] The
book is appropriate here because the crisis-situation in literature
certainly has an apocalyptic tenor. For Kermode, literature in its quest
for meaning is always in a revisionary posture,[10] and is always a
"making sense" of the world.[11] Literature attempts to offer solution to
the human crisis that results from our living always in the "middest,"
that time between middle and end that leaves us without foundation and
without conclusion and is therefore meaningless. We desire some
"intelligible ends" to our crises, and it is narrative's desire to give such
an end, a solution, to us. Kermode writes, "We cannot, of course, be
denied an end; it is one of the great charms of books that they have to
end."[12] The end need not be preexistent, that is, known or decided
before revealed. Narrative is discovery, and fictions do change, even

within themselves. Fictions change to offer yet another solution to
yet another existential crisis, and seek to discover a moment of rest in
which solution is given to the crisis that controls the "middest."

This solution, I suggest, is meaning for human existence that
shows itself as a virtue for living the good life. Solution need not be
truth; it need only be paradigmatic. Other meaning will be sought for
other crises. Narrative simply calls for a "conditional assent" to the
meaning portrayed in the particular situation. Narrative's meanings
change; the virtue revealed changes, and our response and acceptance of
an otherness portrayed by narrative change. This otherness is tested by
experience; therefore, narrative becomes the persistent reexamining and
redefining of otherness. Narrative becomes a process of religious
definition.

II

Narrative technique is not disconnected pieces of a puzzle that
when connected reveal a whole and complete pattern. Rather, narrative
technique and structure mold and shape the pieces themselves only to
discover, perhaps with some degree of astonishment, the completed
pattern that the narrative produces.[13] Narratives are like grammars, or
what Robert Scholes calls, "linguistic possibilities."[14] Of course,
technique is a "catch-all" term. But as Mark Schorer points out,
"technique is the only means he [the author] has of discovering,
exploring, developing his subject, of conveying its meaning, and
finally, of evaluating it."[15] The authors with the best technique offer
the best fiction and, as Schorer says, "will discover more."[16]

Narrative technique has a religious function because it involves
itself with the discovery of value. This value takes on religious
significance because it is an assertion of authority and because it asks
the reader to believe. Authority and belief are central elements of any
religious act. Technique and structure in fiction are more than simply
the organization of materials. Technique is an arrangement of language
which is--by extension--an evaluation of experience. Erich Kahler goes
even further to suggest that reality changes in the narrative act as
outward is taken inward, digested critically, then imposed on the
outward.[17] Indeed, experience is essential to narrative structure. Ortega
y Gasset explains: "To comprehend anything human, be it personal or
collective, one must tell its history."[18] To tell one's history is an act
of narration. The structure of fiction is a type of planned spontaneity
that provides for forms or categories for exploring, questioning, and

defining existence. Technique is, therefore, an evaluative act that plods deftly towards unknown conclusions and unexpected endings.[19]

There is a moment of discovery in the novel that dominates all other moments. Technique, in its process of evaluating experience, reveals a virtue that stands out from and, in its ability to solve crisis, supersedes all other virtues revealed by the novel. This virtue would be the novel's claim for what Kenneth Burke calls "equipment to live by." A world-view is established, a religious world-view that centers on this virtue. Crites suggests that "narrative form is so integral to experience that a figure encountered in a story may choose its moment to manifest itself in the 'world' of our life experience as well."[20] The novel makes the assertion that to live the good life, a person must have faith in something, courage to face something, or confidence in or relation to someone.

One may raise the question, "With such dependence on literary technique, when does author manipulation step aside and the text take control of itself?" I suggest that each works in response to the other. Literature involves what Schorer calls "manipulation,"[21] but at some point the text makes requirements of its author. Content cannot be subsumed into form.[22]

Flannery O'Connor writes about her well known short story, "Good Country People":

> When I started writing that story, I didn't know there was going to be a Ph. D. with a wooden leg in it. I merely found myself one morning writing a description of two women that I knew some-thing about, and before I realized it, I had equipped one of them with a daughter with a wooden leg. As the story progressed, I brought in a Bible salesman, but I had no idea what I was going to do with him. I didn't know he was going to steal that wooden leg until ten or twelve lines before he did it, but when I found out that this was what was going to happen, I realized that it was inevitable. This is a story that produces a shock for the reader, and I think one reason for this is that it produced a shock for the writer.[23]

O' Connor goes on to explain that little rewriting was done to complete the story, and that the story was "under control" throughout the writing. Nonetheless, at times the story "controlled" O'Connor. Technique is discovery for author and reader and ultimately makes evaluative claims about experience that author and particularly reader either accept or reject. Schorer points out that technique is a "deep and primary operation" and "not only that technique *contains* intellectual and moral implications, but it *discovers* them."[24] I would add that virtue is not simply implied but stands at the focal point of most modern literature. Any evaluation or critical analysis of a text's discovered virtue is inseparable from critical analysis of the text's structure.

Finally, technique is religious because it addresses the human situation, which is why character is the critical element of structure in narrative fiction. As Scholes points out, "The interesting roles in fiction are those that are called into being by the predication, the active roles of contractor, judge, and especially the tester."[25] These acts are the functions of character. The narrative element of character is that place in technique that exhibits evaluative comments about human experience. The character in fiction puts to good or bad use those virtues revealed and discovered through narrative technique. Other elements of narrative structure are profoundly important in supporting and interpreting character and character's dimensions. Plot itself, says Brooks, "is a form of understanding and explanation."[26] But it is character, the human creature, that makes the most demanding evaluative claims on human experience. Obviously, I am committed to a psychological conception of character that would be rejected immediately by persons like Alain Robbe-Grillet. I shall have more to say about character and other elements of narrative in the next section on narrative elements. I simply add here that I see at no point an instance where, as Rimmon-Kenan suggests, characters "can be usefully discussed at some distance from their context."[27]

If narrative is motivated by desire for meaningful, human existence--an almost Faustian sense of completion to life--technique is the process by which meaningful existence is revealed. Narrative technique makes evaluative judgments about existence that establishes particular virtues that one may follow to lead the good life. A way of looking at narrative technique is to examine closely those elements that form basic narrative, to explore how each is religious, and to demonstrate how each plays an important role in the discovery of virtue.

III

I shall examine now the four basic elements of narrative structure: tone, atmosphere, plot, and character.[28] Each by nature of its function in the narrative act has religious overtones and significance. I do not suggest that one understands these narrative elements only from a religious perspective. Yet each element possesses by function the potential of religious description and meaning. Narrative elements have, according to Wesley Kort, "a natural relation to corresponding moments in religious life and thought."[29] Each element of narrative points to, discovers, and interprets a religious world-view. Therefore, to understand how narrative leads to religious decision-making and the discovery of virtue, one must understand how narrative elements work in the text and what are their religious significances.

Wesley Kort suggests that narrative's religious nature arises out of a variety of perspectives. From the artist's point of view, the text exhibits a strong sense of situation and establishes an identity over against something else. As metaphor, the text struggles with the burden of revelation, the hidden and revealed act. The text brings about a community between artist and reader by creating an ordered sense of time. Language is oriented toward the inexpressible. From the reader's point of view, a reader with religious sensibilities discovers newness that creates a tension between an old way of life and life's possibilities. The reader accepts the authority of the text. The reader must believe in the world of the text or the act of reading becomes futile. These functions of narrative from artist's and reader's points of view, says Kort, are religious functions.[30]

Kort is correct in his observations about the religious nature of narrative. Where I disagree with his work is when Kort says that the narrative and particularly the narrative elements, draw to themselves associations of religious importance.[31] I suggest that narrative elements reveal religious importance not merely by nature in text but by function within text. Kort is, by admission, reader oriented. I prefer to see reader and text inextricably bound to one another.

Each narrative element plays an instrumental role in the establishing of religious meaning and in turn a world-view. Yet the element of character plays the most essential part in the revealing of a dominant virtue that arises out of decision-making within the text. Characters make choices; characters then live according to the choices they make. Other narrative elements, tone, atmosphere, plot, assist importantly in bringing a character to religious decision. But the character establishes a virtue and a world-view by existential choice. Character's function is to discover what Kort calls the "moral fiber"[32] of fiction. I turn now to a brief definition of these narrative elements, along with a discussion of their religious function. Each element plays a significant role in the interpretation of character in the novels I discuss: tone, in the work by Agee; plot, in the work by Percy; atmosphere, in the work by Warren.

Tone

The tone of a text suggests a number of possibilities: point of view, language, style, voice. To have a story is to have a storyteller. The storyteller fashions a world, an ethos. He/She creates a situation that allows for discovery. Tone is the narrative element that deals perhaps the most with the ineffable. Paul Ricoeur explains that the voice of the text is involved "in the problems of communication."[33] Whether the narrator is omniscient, unreliable, writes in stream of consciousness, or whether the narrator is the author him/herself or a character in the story, he/she creates a sense, a feeling that invites such subjective observations like trust or wariness, optimism or pessimism, expectation or resignation.

Tone is the relationship that exists between author and narrative. The critic cannot separate the story from the teller of the story. Tone takes on an almost confessional nature. The author cannot hide his/her subjective presence in the story. Tone has the quality that Henry James calls "the focus of narration," "the commanding centre," "the means through which intensity, vividness, coherence, and economy of treatment could be achieved."[34] Percy Lubbock in *The Craft of Fiction* argues that, "The whole intricate question of method, in the craft of fiction, I take to be governed by the question of the relation in which the narrator stands to the story."[35] I agree to a point, yet believe that the tone of the story is more than simply the narrator's stance in relation to the text, as Lubbock suggests.

Tone has a religious meaning and function. Anything foundational, any belief which is one's "commanding centre" in one's world-view, is religious. Yet tone is more than point of view. Rather, and Kort is correct here, tone asks that we accept someone else's world-- what Giles Gunn calls the "hypothetical creation" by fiction[36]--if only for a short while. The granting of such authority, I suggest, is a religious act committed by the reader but required by tone. The critic grants the text autonomy. Tone is what informs and creates the text's autonomous world which the reader is willing, at least momentarily, to accept. Kort explains that "tone brings into the fictional world the quality of beliefs,"[37] and I suggest that this quality is a religious attitude toward the newly discovered world in the text.

Atmosphere

Atmosphere discovers and establishes boundaries in the narrative. The establishing of limits and boundaries is also an religious act.

Other words for atmosphere are scene, setting, scope, dimension. Atmosphere involves the creation of a credible environment in which the action of the narrative takes place. Atmosphere, according to Kort, "determines the range of possibilities or the conditions by or under which the fictional world is constituted."[38] Characters within fiction cannot change atmosphere; authors must be consistent to an atmosphere throughout the text. The atmosphere is a result of the creative efforts of the author and evolves out of narrative technique.

Atmosphere is established as the novel progresses. Characters may gain awareness of their finitude. Time reveals itself as relentless and imposed. Stephen Crane's Maggie is controlled by her environment; she can become nothing other than a prostitute. Environment is a favorite element--an atmosphere--of the naturalist writers. Wesley Kort suggests that atmosphere takes on three characteristics in novels. Landscape can be self-defining. Hardy's Wessex country or Faulkner's Yoknapatawpha County are good examples. Atmosphere can be those finite conditions that threaten human life--death and disease. I would go even further and suggest that language is limiting and requires unavoidable acts on the parts of character.[39]

Atmosphere is limiting and establishes boundaries and parameters with which a piece of fiction must remain constant. Eudora Welty in *Place In Fiction* describes atmosphere as "delicate control" over character.[40] Characters have no decision over the time and the place to which they belong. Characters respond to the limitations imposed by atmosphere and discover possibilities for living the good life. While the atmosphere of the text "lies beyond the borders of human attention,"[41] how characters exhibit themselves in light of limited understanding and control tells the reader something about the characters and the characters something about self-identity. Characters often discover the virtuous life by accepting and/or challenging the limitations of atmosphere or by confronting the otherness that atmosphere suggests by its transcendence of human control.

Plot

Peter Brooks claims that what shapes narrative is "the play of desire in time that makes us turn pages and strive towards narrative's ends."[42] I agree that the fundamental motivation of narrative is desire for completion and end, "a line of intention and a portent of design that hold the promise of progress toward meaning."[43] Todorov calls plot a desire, within the text, for "equilibrium."[44] And for Brooks plot is the principle of design and "intention,"[45] the "organizing dynamic" of a text.[46] Plot, like each element of narrative, is involved with discovery of meaning, a "form of understanding and explanation."[47] Plot's religious significance in narrative is that plot is the prime mover of narrative towards wholeness. Plot takes fragmented moments of action and creates order. Plot takes open-ended situations and brings them to a close. While these actions are not unique to religion, they do have religious implications.

Plot's desire for closure is noticeably apocalyptic.[48] Narrative begins with an established moment in time. Rising action follows. A crisis moment is revealed followed by recognition of crisis and some re-establishment of a more stable time, and plot, by nature, say Robert Macauley and George Lanning, "leads most powerfully toward . . . moral judgment." *Denoument* demands a sorting-out of life; a plot cannot end without the assigning of value."[49] Once plot assigns values, a character then chooses to accept or reject them. Thus a character's action and development is highly dependent on the plot. The plot establishes context within which character makes virtue-revealing decisions.

Kermode sees the religious intention of plot related to the human amazement with time.[50] The world lacks order and meaning. Narrative plot imposes order and meaning on a fictive world. Kort argues that "plots are not so much imposed as they are evoked, and the time which they reflect is not so much linear as it is repetitious."[51] The plot for Kort is repeatable time in the same sense as Eliade's notion of the eternal return. A plot is ritual and repetitive and allows for a moment of return to a time that is stable and meaningful and that sets one free from the chaos and the meaninglessness of the present.

A character chooses the ritual moments of immersion into a tradition that allows for cleansing and, in turn, meaningful existence. The plot is supportive of a character by providing those repetitive moments in which the character can make decisions that establish a virtue by which he/she will live. The plot provides a framework for character existence. The provision of a guiding framework is perhaps plot's most religious function.

Character

Ira Konigsberg writes that the novel's "capacity to interest and convince us is dependent upon its creation of the probable and relevant."[52] I agree, and suggest that the narrative element of character is what gives the novel its relevance. A character in narrative intensifies our own self-awareness if for no other reason than we are relating to lives and interpreting ourselves in relation to these lives. Characters are not real; to claim otherwise is naive. Higbie is explicit. To make the claim that a character is "real" is to preclude literary analysis. "It provides no terms to use and even denies that there are a text and a response to analyze."[53] The characters within a text are first and foremost elements of the text.

Within the text the characters are what they do. They act within the framework of plot and are interpreted and described in relation to tone and atmosphere. But if a text is to have any religious implications, focus must be on a character who by discovery and choice of virtue establishes the text's world-view. "No function can be defined unless it is attributed to some character," says Ricoeur.[54]

Desire as motivation for narrative is critical in the development of character. Character is an agent in the text that is acting out fulfillment of desires. I define characters in much the same way as Higbie does, "in terms of their verb . . . they are ways of doing--acting and being acted upon."[55] Thus characters may assume two roles in the text, agent or patient. Perhaps the character is in control of self and initiates the movement towards fulfillment of desire. Perhaps the character is acted upon by some outside force to which he/she must respond to fulfill desire. In either place, the character must actively make decisions about how to live in the world or how to respond to the world. As the character acts to structure his/her experience within the world, a world-view is created.

When this world-view takes on a value structure in the form of a particular virtue that supersedes all other virtues, a religious world-view is formed. Narrative always brings character to religious decision making that establishes this dominant virtue. The character need not live according to the established world-view. The virtue that creates the world-view is merely discovered and presented and can either be accepted or rejected by character or reader. But it is the character, says Ricoeur, "who mediates the quest."[56]

The narrative element of character has religious significance because existential crises always confront characters and provide a situation in which virtue-establishing decisions are made. Characters desire order and control and are faced--throughout narrative--with opportunity to gain or to lose control of their existences. And there always exists a critical point in narrative when decision reaches crisis stage. Stephen Crites calls it the "decisive episode in the story, its moment of crisis between the past remembered and the future anticipated but still undetermined."[57] The "undetermined" is character's decision that leads to discovery.

The character element is religious because within the hypothetical world of the text, narrative presents a character with myriad possibilities for him/her to choose good and bad. The character in a text suggests potential for good and evil according to the decision he/she makes. A character is not merely an element placed within a pre-structured world; rather, a character creates the novel's world.

Most important, the character addresses the critical question of self-identity. The essential desire of character in the novel is to discover an answer to the question, "Who am I?" Such a question is replete with religious implications and for the literary critic unavoidable implications. The quest for self-identity invites exploration into human nature, its malleability and possibility, and has social as well as personal implications. Implicit in the question of self-identity is the human being's relationship to the world.

The narrative element of character addresses the issue of belief and authority. Critical to my thesis and demonstrated in my analysis of the fiction I have chosen is the idea that a character in fiction actively seeks some authority which informs the very nature of human existence. A character comes to the point in the text where acquiescence is made to a particular virtue in which the character places all authority for existence and therefore leads the good life because of his/her choice.

Belief and authority are critical to establishing a religious world-view. The authors I discuss describe acts of belief by their characters in which virtue is discovered and authority is granted to it. Agee's characters discover *philia* and place an implicit trust in the world of human relationship. Percy's characters discover faith and grant authority to God for the transformation and reconciliation of the world. Warren's characters believe courage is the answer in a world unpredictable and tragically impositional.

IV

I wish now to give a brief description of the religious world-views I believe reflect the characters' discoveries and choices in the novels critical to my study. By no means are these religious world-views the only ones encountered in fiction or society for that matter.[58] These world views do reflect dominant religious world-views in Western thought today. All belief defies categories, but most religious thought can be placed under the rubrics of a theology of relatedness, a transcendent theology, or a tragic theology, or, at least, some mixture of the three. I keep the categories distinct for purposes of clearer explication. Following each chapter of critical analysis of the literary text, I suggest a prominent theological/religious thinker who "fits" within one of the categories and show how his work relates to the religious world-view discovered to be at work in the novel. For Agee I have chosen William James and his relational theology, for Percy, Saint Augustine and his transcendental theology. For Warren I have chosen Paul Tillich and his religious view of tragedy.

A theology of relatedness, to some degree, has its modern origins in Romanticism but is given its most profound expression at the turn of the century in the social gospel of Walter Rauschenbusch and the therapeutic psychology of persons like William James. Rauschenbusch was well versed in the works of Albrect Ritschl and Washington Gladden and, without doubt, William James read the works of all three men. These persons were convinced that with enough mental and physical labor persons could live together harmoniously in a world full of the strife of the creature's own making. Important in this theology is a basic trust in the world to provide for one's care. Adolph Harnack echoes the sentiments of the period with his classical statement about the "Fatherhood of God and brotherhood of man." There is a certain irony in the explicit sexism of the comment. Nonetheless, for the period, it did emphasize the family which was the microcosm of the world at large. Wilhelm Reich suggests in the early twentieth century that the family is the external world.[59] And, of course, Rauschenbusch is trying to build the family of God into the Kingdom of God on earth by urging persons to love one another with a familial love. The kingdom is the "realm of love"[60] organized under the "fellowship of humanity."[61]

James is advocating a relational theology that is founded on honesty, trust, and the support of one human creature for another. The spiritual as well as physical survival of the human creature is dependent on community, a familial relationship that requires mutual interdependence between its members for productive and happy survival in the world. I have chosen James and his explication of relational theology to give religious ground for Agee's notion of *philia* in *A Death in the Family*.

Transcendent theology suggests that one cannot trust the world and that the *communitas* advocated by relational theology is not achievable. In fact, the human creature is unable, alone, to create any cohesiveness in a world fallen and evil. This view is strong through Christian tradition, the two cities of Saint Augustine, the vision of

Dante, the leap of Kierkegaard, the angry God of Jonathan Edwards, and the immoral society of Reinhold Niebuhr. Because one cannot trust the world, one must look outside the world for a transcendent whole, God, to bring meaning to a fragmented and meaningless world. Faith is the necessary virtue that sustains the person in a world alienated from God.

I have chosen Saint Augustine's *Civitas Dei* to illustrate Percy's understanding of the virtue of faith and his insistence on a trust in a world not of this world. The emphasis here is transcendence; persons are helpless on their own and require an otherness outside of self and world to bring purpose to existence.

A theory of tragedy suggests that the human creature is limited by nature and existence. We are frightened by our mortality and anxious over what little freedom we do possess. We have very little control over the two most significant events of our lives, birth and death, and yet we are responsible to each. Who we are, self-identity, is molded by those choices in life we necessarily have to make. Often life involves conflict of choices. There are no right and wrong choices, merely choice, for which we are responsible. Choices are necessary because while we cannot trust the world, we must live in the world. We feel guilt because we know we can be better than we are, and we fear death because it represents the unknown to us.

Tragic theology suggests that we are responsible for the bit of integrity we can get from life. The world is careless with its inhabitants yet we carry on with life in spite of an existence that thwarts us at every turn for reasons, more often than not, unknown to us. To live so precariously requires courage. The courageous act is to accept one's precarious existence, one's guilt, one's finitude and to make meaning out of one's limited existence.

I choose Paul Tillich to illustrate Warren's understanding of the virtue courage in *A Place to Come To.* Like Warren, Tillich believes that courageous living alone, "the courage to be," allows one to endure and make meaning in a world that threatens us with our own tragic limitations. Persons can be noble and maintain their integrity in the unavoidably tragic dimension of life. To demonstrate my claims about the nature and function of narrative, the role of virtue in the lives of narratives' characters, and the religious world-view each narrative establishes, let us now turn to the practical analyses of the literary texts.

CHAPTER 2

FROM HOLE TO WHOLE:
JAMES AGEE'S *A DEATH IN THE FAMILY*

James Agee's novel, *A Death in the Family*,[1] describes the enduring strength of the human family and the spiritual development of family members in the face of tragedy. Agee's is a positive view of the world. Indeed, terrible and tragic events do take place in persons' lives, but no event is so tragic that it cannot be withstood and endured by relying on substantive religious models and particularly on the nurture and support of relationships--family relationships. By religious model, I mean those relational metaphors for God, father, friend, king, liberator, used by traditional Judaism and Christianity to suggest a personal relationship with the Holy.[2] By family, I mean simply those immediate and extended persons related by marriage or biology. Agee believes that acts of *philia*, familial love, can make good out of bad and can lend stability and purpose to a world often confusing and unpredictable. Family is the most secure and predictable, as well as the most religious, event in one's life.

Agee's characters come to believe that familial friendship holds the possibilities for human beings to live the good life. Persons need a connectedness to family in order to confront and to endure life's bad times. Agee portrays human beings who experience a world ambivalent and difficult and who somehow maintain healthy souls and minds by a most difficult task of loving one another--the virtue *philia*. This sounds old fashioned, and it is. Dwight MacDonald says that the theme of *A Death in the Family*, "is the confrontation of love . . . carried to its highest possible reach, and death, as the negation of life and yet a necessary part of it."[3] While Salinger is describing arduous rites of passage and Hemingway the tragic hero who must endure the world's pain without even love, Agee is suggesting that there remains room for sacrificial, vicarious love and human communion in a world where individuals fight for autonomy.

A Death in the Family is about a family's traumatic experience of losing one of its members, and the experience, says Robert Coles, is "an occasion not for psychological collapse or for growth in response to a crisis but rather for an unfolding of grace in both old and young. A family is able to regard itself rather closely and feel blessed as well as stricken badly."[4] Yet the trauma allows for more than an "unfolding of grace." Family members are also able to move from a father-centered world where characters depend--perhaps too much--on the father, to a relational world where family members depend on one another and, at the same time, establish individual autonomy. Characters are able to move from a spiritual myopia within a God-the-Father-centered world to a spiritual independence that reveals the most profound religious model to be the family matrix.

Characters, in Agee's novel, are brought to the point of making these critical, self-defining choices when faced with the tragic event of a death in the family, the death of the father. The father's death is the narrative's crisis-event to which characters within the narrative structure are required to respond. The father's death is the "existential crisis." Characters must now discover a solution to the crisis. The father, until his death, was the family's center of strength, emotionally and physically. Death removes the center and leaves an absence or hole in the lives of the family members. Characters must now seek wholeness to fill the emptiness left by the father's death. I suggest that major characters in Agee's text fall into two categories. One category is characters who cannot overcome the loss of the father from the center of their world and/or who remain so committed to the notion of the father-centered world that no sense of family or acts of *philia* play an essential role in their lives. These persons are sorely insecure and alienated from meaning. Their lives exhibit a critical absence of purpose and direction. The other category is characters who move beyond the father-centered world and establish, with the love and nurture of family, a new direction and meaning for existence. No longer defined by the father at the center of their lives, they take charge of their lives and make meaning in the world through acts of *philia*. These characters go through emotional and spiritual transition, from dependence on a father within a father-centered world-view, to independence and self-reliance within a relational world-view.

The father, Jay Follet, leaves a tragic and profound emptiness--a "hole"--in the lives of the Follet family members because they have come to be so dependent on him. Yet while Jay's death is a tremendous loss for the family members, with his death family members also experience emotional and spiritual gain. Characters go from " a hole to a whole," becoming more complete, self-confident, and most important, relational human beings. They become less dependent on *a* person and more dependent on self and one another. From a hierarchy of the father at the top, characters move to a matrix with family members all around. Instead of a critical center occupied by the father, where character knows meaning only through extension from center, characters now create and discover meaning, become spiritually and emotionally whole, by acts of *philia* toward one another.

But the death of the father represents far more than a family crisis in the lives of the novel's characters. The death of the father also represents a spiritual crisis and is a metaphor for the death of God the Father as a religious model. The model of God the Father fails as a way of looking at the world religiously and therefore must be discarded by particular characters. In its place a new model of ultimacy must be established if these persons are to have any ground of being. The narrative elements tone and character most profoundly reveal the religious dimensions of the Agee story. And these elements of narrative structure serve well to reveal that *philia*--familial friendship--is a critical and prominent virtue of the Agee text.

I

Agee is aware of the significance of tone for the literary text. An application for a Guggenheim Fellowship in 1937 had as one of his goals, to write serious stories "whose whole intention is the direct communication of the intensity of common experience."[5] Tone is for Agee what Macauley and Lanning describe as "a matter of angles--the angle or angles from which a story is seen."[6] Tone is a critical narrative dimension of Agee's novel.

The tone in *A Death in the Family* reveals the very profound nature of the family's loss of its father. The pathos of the situation is severe, and we are aware of a visible hole left at the center of the lives of the family members. We sense the total dependence a family has on its father. The novel begins with a number of instances in which the father demonstrates his pivotal and critical role in the family. There is the father's relationship with his son, Rufus. They walk home from an evening out, stop and sit on a large rock. The feeling is one of "complete contentment . . . in the feeling that they were reconciled, that there was really no division, no estrangement, or none so strong, anyhow, that it could mean much, by comparison with the unity that was so firm and assured, here" (26). Jay is Rufus' role-model, his mentor, and is at the center of his son's existence. Rufus' security and serenity depend on his "unity" with his father. Separation from his father would be emotionally catastrophic.

Jay's wife, Mary, exhibits similar dependence on the father/husband of the family. She is an extension of her husband, finding pleasure only in his pleasure, meaning only in his meaning. For breakfast, she fixes eggs the way he likes them and not the way she likes them. She makes his coffee the way he likes it and not the way she likes it. Jay returns her loyalty. The morning before Jay's death, at breakfast, they do not "take their eyes from each other . . . they had nothing to say. They were not disturbed by this, but both felt almost the shyness of courtship" (40-41). Mary knows only the ideal family life provided by Jay. With Jay's death, she must seek strength from other sources to help her through her tragedy.

Tone is established. The angle of vision taken by author, character, and reader suggests that the father is the heart of the Follet family. The text asks us to believe that Jay Follet is indispensable to the unity and wholeness of this family and that his death would be the most tragic and significant event to happen to the Follets. Yet the tone of the text after the father's death changes. True, the loss of a father is tragic and leaves a hole in the lives of family members. Yet tone also suggests that there is gain in the lives of the members of the family. Characters become more independent and develop a greater sense of self, emotionally and religiously.

Thus while pathos is extreme when Jay is killed in an automobile accident, characters now seek and discover a way(s) out of this despair. Tone, once pathetic, becomes hopeful, as characters choose to be supportive of one another in the face of tragedy. Characters who choose family friendship, *philia*, to replace the absent father, will somehow make their lives whole and productive again. Mary, Jay's wife, now exclaims, "I am meeting it face to face, I am living through it" (283), certainly a declaration of independence. Rufus, the young boy, is finally able to say: "Dead. He's dead. That's what he is; he's dead" (297). The acknowledgement of his father's death allows Rufus, with support of family, to get on with a productive life.

II

Rufus, Jay's son, and Ralph, Jay's brother, must deal with the literal loss of a center, a hole, left in their lives by Jay's death. Rufus, because of his youth, (he is only six) and Ralph, because of his emotional immaturity, are capable only of understanding the physical absence brought by the father's death. Both characters had become debilitatingly dependent on Jay. Rufus will overcome the unhealthy dependence he had on his father and discover a family matrix of love and support that will bring new meaning to his life. Ralph will remain insecure and isolated from family because he fails to let go of his crippling need for Jay.

Ralph Follet is the most tragic character in *A Death in the Family*; he has no sense of self or community and is estranged from family. He is obsessively dependent on Jay. Of course Jay is responsible, to some degree, for Ralph's dependence. He is always giving in to Ralph's requests. A typical conversation occurs between the two men the day of Jay's death and is quite revealing. Jay gets a call from Ralph saying that their father is dying, and that Jay must come home. Jay suspects that Ralph is lying; he has exaggerated their father's condition before, and he responds to Ralph's call with what Agee describes as "tight rage" (31). Jay wants to "hit him" (32), and begins to feel "disgust for himself, for haggling about it" with Ralph, and therefore says to Ralph, "I'll be right along" (33). Jay's disgust and rage suggest that he is aware of Ralph's dependence, yet against better judgment does nothing about it.

Ralph's inability to fill the void left by Jay's death comes from his guilt that he is somehow responsible for his brother's death. He made the call that required the car trip that resulted in Jay's accident. Ralph had lied about their father's condition simply to get Jay to come. Yet guilt is nothing new to Ralph's life, for his alcoholism and inability to look after the ill father have plagued him with guilt for some time.

Yet Ralph's lack of family connection and his emotional instability are the most dominant factors in his inability to put Jay's death in perspective. He is childish and lives a very self-centered existence. "Everything he did, every tone his voice took, was controlled by his idea of what would make the best impression on others" (71). When confronted by responsibility or the possibility of a strong familial relationship, Ralph retreats into a self-centeredness. His inability to cope with the ambiguities and tragedies of the real world are expressed by his exclamation in response to his ineptitude to cope with his father's illness, "But I'm not a man. I'm a baby" (72). Alienated from family, Ralph is no more than a "baby." He is powerless and dependent and lacks the family structure to give purpose and direction to his life. Ralph, unable to cope with his father's illness, will never be able to cope with the death of the person on whom he has become totally dependent. After Jay's death, Ralph makes his only attempt at *philia*, but his act is too little too late. He is an undertaker, and when Jay dies, offers to do the funeral for nothing; he has no love to offer. Ralph makes one last futile attempt to extract meaning from Jay's life. Unfortunately, he is the dead offering to bury the dead.

Rufus' dependence on his father is different from Ralph's. His is a six year old boy's love of father. Rufus can do nothing other than depend on his father. While his loss seems far more tragic than Ralph's, Rufus acknowledges the death of his father, the tragic and painful loss it represents for his life, and learns to live a more meaningful existence.

We are aware of the critical role that Jay plays in Rufus' life. Rufus is an extension of his father and finds self-definition in their relationship. In fact, their relationship is somewhat ideal, the near perfect father-son relationship. Each is included intimately in the other's life. Jay decides, as they saunter through the night, that he will "hoist . . . a couple" of beers (23) at the local bar. Rufus swells with pride and feels a "warmth of love" as his father proudly says "that's my boy . . . six years old, and he can already read like I couldn't read when I was twice his age" (23-4). They leave the bar and continue to walk home, stopping in a vacant lot where they sit, without words, and simply enjoy the presence of one another. They find sustenance in their relationship, and they are comfortable with one another's presence. They suck "Life Savers" (24), an act which emphasizes the vitality of their relationship. Agee describes the sense of the young boy as he and his father sit on a large rock in the open lot as that of "complete contentment" (26). For a few fleeting moments father and son know no conflict. Their relationship is almost transcendent, certainly symbiotic. All meaning for Rufus is found in his father. The loss of his father will leave a profound and meaningless hole in his life.

Coles tells us that Agee's view of human nature "is a wry and detached view, but one also informed by a mixture of awe and sadness-- awe that in the face of so many hurdles the child often comes out rather sturdy, and sadness that those hurdles do indeed exact their toll."[7] The death of Jay Follet exacts a tremendous toll on young Rufus. He matures as the novel progresses, to the extent a six year old can. Perhaps, at best, Rufus develops sensitivity to the meaning and the lack of meaning in the world. He does discover that in the face of such a crisis, meaning is found only in relation to family.

The morning following his father's death, he rushes into the room calling, "Daddy! Daddy!" (235) He wants to show his father the new cap Aunt Hannah bought him the day before. Because his father is his

center of meaning, Rufus wants his approval for even the most minor
of things. Rufus questions his mother to the whereabouts of his father
only to get the perfunctory answer, "He's gone away to heaven . . .
Because God wanted him" (237). But Rufus knows dead; he has seen
the rabbits killed by the dogs, and he asks, "Is Daddy dead" (237)? Yet
Rufus does not quite understand; he senses a loss but cannot articulate
it. He is kept out of school and this makes him feel special. When he
encounters a group of young boys outside of his house, he tells them:
"My Daddy's dead" (255). He is certain that they will think "well" of
him and prepares to tell the young boys his story. He feels the "sober
air . . . charged with [the] great energy and with a sense of glory and of
danger" (254). Rufus tells his story but finds he is not so special.
The young children are cruel and exclaim, falsely, that if his daddy had
not been drunk, he would be alive today. Rufus begins to realize that it
is not so special to have a dead father, and the meaninglessness of the
world is slowly thrust upon him. He begins to feel a great loss.

Rufus returns home attempting to reclaim some memory of his
father, the most critical figure in his family life.

> He looked at his father's morsechair . . . with a sense of
> deepstealth and secrecy he finally went over and stood
> beside it . . . He smelled   of the chair . . . There was
> only the cold smell of tobacco and, high   along   the
> back, a   faint   smell of hair. He thought of the ash tray
> on its weighted strap on the arm; it was empty. He ran
> his finger inside it; there was only a dim smudge of ash .
> . . He   looked at his finger for a moment and licked it;
> his tongue tasted of darkness (265).

Rufus feels alone and powerless. His mother had avoided the
issue of his father's death. The young boy has nowhere to turn for
explanation and direction. Under different circumstances, he could turn
to his father. Rufus goes to view his father's body for the last time.
He observes his father's body, "the arch of the nose" and "the still
strong mouth . . . but most of all" a look of "indifference" (289).
Rufus thinks to himself: "Dead. He's dead. That's what he is; he's
dead" (297). The admission on Rufus' part brings very little new
understanding; he will need family's help for this. He simply
articulates what he has been feeling all along, a sense of emptiness and
fragmentation and that the world can be mysteriously cruel and
meaningless.

But meaning is inherent in the world as well. Andrew, Mary's
agnostic brother, invites Rufus for a walk following the funeral. He

wants to tell Rufus about the funeral which Rufus was not allowed to
attend. The language is full of inconsistencies for the six year old boy,
words about love and hate. Andrew hates the priest who performs the
funeral; "That son of a bitch, " Andrew said, "He said he couldn't read
the complete burial service over your father because your father had
never been baptized . . . Some church, he snarled, and they call
themselves Christians" (316). Andrew is aware that the church has
failed in its familial obligation. The family of God has not treated one
of its members like family. But he tells Rufus more, something
"miraculous, magnificent" (315). A giant butterfly lights on Jay's
coffin as he is lowered into the ground. The butterfly remains on the
coffin until it reaches the bottom of the grave and, then, flies upward.
At the same time, the sun breaks out from behind the clouds in the sky
and shines brilliantly, "dazzling bright." "If there are any such things
as miracles," says Andrew, "then that's surely miraculous" (314-5).
And Rufus' uncle goes on to talk about God in a way "he had never
heard his uncle speak of God except as if he disliked Him" (312).

I suggest that Agee's concluding paragraphs are too staged, and
that the butterfly sequence is simply too good, but I also suggest that
the butterfly sequence is not the central point. Rather, Agee wishes to
emphasize the relationship between Andrew and Rufus. Andrew must
tell his story to someone and is searching blindly to grasp some
understanding of Jay's death. Earlier he had suggested that it should
have been he that died. He tells his story to Rufus, slowly and
deliberately to give it order. Rufus "breathed in a deep breath of pride
and love" because his uncle told this story "to him" (315). Rufus does
not understand the mixed messages Andrew is passing on; he hates the
church, and he hates members of the family for allowing the church to
use Jay in this fashion (315). But Andrew loves Jay and now expresses
his love for Rufus. Andrew and Rufus seek explanation, an answer to
questions raised by Jay's death. Yet the only answer is that reason
provides no answer to death. Andrew will find no answers to explain
the death, but he will find meaning in the experience of "relating" to the
young Rufus and the family that awaits him at home. Andrew and
Rufus have only each other and the other family members. And
realizing this, Andrew says, "'It's time to go home,' and all the way
home they walked in silence" (318).

Home becomes a symbol for order and meaning because home is
the place of family. Andrew's sense of a "creative" and "redeeming" act
begins with the incident of the butterfly, for a long time a symbol of
the Christian resurrection. But his affirmation and articulation of any

religious experience comes through his relationship, though tenuous, with the young Rufus and the family to which they return "all the way home in silence." Rufus has discovered a friend, and to some degree, the hole left by the death of his father is filled by Andrew's act of *philia*. Rufus' gain is not so obvious. Yet acknowledgement of his father's death is an assertion of independence and an act of self-awareness. Because of tragic and unfortunate circumstances, Rufus no longer depends on his father for self-definition. He is free to discover and choose meaning through the family matrix.

III

Two of Agee's characters, Father Jackson and Mary, demonstrate a religious dependence on God the Father. For them, Jay's death becomes a metaphor for spiritual crisis. Father Jackson represents a traditional view of the church. God relates to individuals in a fatherly fashion as head of the family of God. But the priest comes across as being too dependent and steeped in tradition to be of any help to the grieving family. In fact, Agee's description of Father Jackson is a rather searing indictment of the family of God, with the Father God as the family's head. Mary represents a break from tradition in which new models for personal relationships with God are sought and found. Jay's death is a tragic loss for Mary but provides opportunity for emotional and spiritual growth. Jay's death is a metaphor for the death of God the Father as model for religious experience and provides Mary with opportunity for spiritual growth, a newly discovered religious independence to couple with her newly discovered personal freedom.

The most sinister character in *A Death in the Family* is Father Jackson. There is much irony in his title of Father. As a spiritual Father, he provides no comfort or nurture when, following Jay's death, he calls on the Follet family. He fails miserably to represent well the family of the church. Agee's description of Jackson is chilling. "He wore a long shallow hat and he had a long, sharp, bluish chin almost like a plow. He carried a small, shining black suitcase. He seemed to be as disconcerted and displeased as they were" (273).

Father Jackson comes ostensibly to nurture the family but brings only greater discomfort. He takes pride in telling Mary that he cannot read the entire burial service for Jay because he was never baptized. The children "could not conceive of what was being done to their mother, but in his own way each was sure that it was something evil, to which she was submitting almost without struggle, and by which she was deceived" (278). The priest believes that he is doing the work of God the Father, but he has become so impersonal and theistic that he has lost his humanity. Indeed, unlike family in Agee's novel, the church, with *Father* Jackson as one of its earthly heads and God the Father as its divine head, practices a certain exclusivity. Agee makes us aware that exclusivity is "something evil." The priest upsets the children by sitting in their dead father's chair and by speaking harshly to them for acting in a way he describes as "uncivil" (276). Catherine's face turns red and Rufus begins "to turn cold in the pit of his stomach" (276).

Father Jackson lacks all the qualities so important to family, particularly *philia*. He is remote, lacking in feeling, "he spoke almost wholly without emphasis and with only the subtlest coloring, as if the personal emotion, the coloring, were cast against the words from a distance, like echoes" (280). Perhaps Agee is suggesting that the idea of God as Father as a metaphor for religious experience has become remote and distant and that such a model no longer speaks to the needs of some people. Certainly, Agee is suggesting that the priest has become blindly dependent on a very cold and rigid understanding of God as Father and Head of the Christian community. Someone so unfeeling and estranged from the concept of family can offer little comfort to a family who is grieving. His impact on the family is to make Mary feel "defeated and entranced" (281).

Andrew's description of the priest after Father Jackson refused to read the entire burial service for Jay is, "that son of a bitch" (316). With such a description, Andrew removes Jackson from the human family. The priest is no better than an animal. His actions are coldly habitual. Father Jackson, whose life and profession are critical to the well-being of a spiritual family, fails to perceive and act on what Agee believes is the most spiritual dimension of the human family, the virtue *philia*.

Mary undergoes the most radical change both personally and religiously in *A Death in the Family* and requires the most in-depth analysis of character in Agee's text. Jay's death is indeed a family crisis for Mary. A happy, almost idyllic family life is disrupted and family life collapses. What will she tell the children? Why did this happen to her? How will she live her life without Jay? She will endure this tragedy. Family restores a sense of stability to her life. Friends and family give of themselves freely and unselfishly, and Mary's loss embodies certain gain. Jay's death remains painful and unfathomable, yet Mary finds courage to endure her situation, an inner strength bolstered by the love of those persons around her, and she will cope with her loss.

Mary's most profound gain is the spiritual independence for which Jay's death serves as a metaphor. The death of the father represents a spiritual crisis and is a metaphor for the death of God the Father as a model for religious expression in Mary's life. The model of God the Father fails Mary in her time of crisis. In its place Mary will seek a new model for religious expression that is grounded in the familial love, *philia*. A close look at the language of the text, as well as at the more firmly entrenched model of God the Father in the religious lives of certain characters, will serve to shed light on our discussion.

Fathers in general, throughout the novel, give Mary a great deal of trouble. Early in the novel we learn that Mary is uneasy with Jay's family, particularly the father who, she says, is the "one barrier between them" (55). There is a certain irony in her dislike of Jay's father. She admits that he is "genuinely kind hearted" even when people "outrageously abused his generosity." But she points out that, "he had never really stood up for her strongly and bravely, and angrily" (54-5). I suggest that Mary begins the novel to some degree aware that the father image offers very little to her in terms of the personal support and nurture she needs as a woman. We shall discover that the Father God metaphor is inadequate for her religious needs.

She finds herself wishing that the old man would die and "no longer stand between me and Jay" (56). Yet it is not easy for Mary to break away from years of dependence on "fathers" and from the significant and formative roles they play in her life. The moment she criticizes Jay's father, a strong sense of guilt envelops her. Ironically, she turns to God the Father for forgiveness: "Lord, cleanse my soul for such abominations" (56).

Mary first rejects "literal" father-figures in her life. She exhibits a degree of self-assertion by wishing the old man dead. But thus far she is unable to make a cosmic projection of her wish and to do the same for God the Father. She continues her prayer of confession, "descend and fill my heart" (56). But her prayer will go unanswered. The "emptiness of heart," she discovers, is a result of the inadequacy and inability of a male-god to speak to her as a woman. Her frustrations will lead to patricide. But for the moment she says, "I must just: trust in God . . . Just: do His will, and put all my trust in Him" (58).

I wish to focus particularly on chapter 8 of the text. Mary's religious development takes on new significance when she is faced with the possible death of her husband, Jay. She receives a phone call saying that her husband has been in an accident; the caller does not tell her if Jay is dead or alive. I find it fascinating that she does not ask. Is the absence of question a result of shock? The caller says that the accident is serious. Perhaps there is some intuitive awareness of her own needs and growth that allows for this act of prescience. Her own response when she realizes that she did not ask is, "I'm simply not going to think about it" (114). The strength required of her, or of anyone, to reject the traditional Father God certainly makes such an assertion plausible.

The phone conversation emphasizes Mary's male-dominated world. "Is there a *man* in *his* family, some kin, who could come out? We'd appreciate if you could send a *man*" (111-2). Mary calls her brother, Andrew, who responds to the news with the exclamation, "Oh, my God, Mary" (112). Of course, the God in the text is the men's God. Mary needs more, so she asks Hannah, an Aunt, to come and stay with her while she awaits news. Her parents live near by, but Mary does not need her mother, who is an extension of her father, nor particularly her father, in this difficult time. Briefly, the text takes on a strange tenor suggesting the firmly entrenched male-idea of woman in contemporary family. Why didn't the caller ask me to come, she asks herself. "No, I'd have to stay with the children . . . My place'd be home anyhow, getting things ready, he knows that" (114). She prepares the bed and room in which Jay will stay.

Suddenly, she feels a strong urge to pray, the passage is poignantly descriptive of her religious condition. Mary positions herself on "her knees," passive and receptive. She "pulled down the shade. She turned out the light." A sense of spiritual darkness casts shadows over her. She seeks liberation from and nurture through the looming tragedy and tries to pray. "O God, if it be Thy will, she whispered" but "could not think of anything more. Thy will be done. And again she could think of nothing more" (115). The language is rich here suggesting her spiritual unknowing. Mary stands from her unfinished prayer. "The water for the tea had *almost* boiled away. The water in the kettle was *scarcely, tepid*. The fire was *almost out*" (115). Each metaphor emphasizes Mary's spiritual emptiness and lack of religious zeal.

Aunt Hannah arrives with Mary's brother Andrew, the family agnostic. His eyes say to Mary, "And you can still believe in that idiotic God of yours" (116)? The answer is no because He was never her God; he is Andrew's. Nonetheless, Mary cannot give up hope that Jay is alive, and therefore some dependency on the Father God. She talks to Aunt Hannah of her expectations of Jay's convalescence. Yet during their discussions, signs throughout the text point to Mary's decreasing dependence on the God the Father model. Again the water boils away. Perhaps she is experiencing a new kind of cleansing, or perhaps, she is losing her baptism. Not totally: she tells Hannah that there is "still plenty for two cups." Yet she looks at the water in the pot and wonders "what the water might possibly be good for" (119).

A change is taking place in Mary, one she cannot fully articulate; nevertheless, the change is real. She is haunted again by not asking Jay's condition when the farmer called. "In heaven's name, why didn't I ask him! Why didn't I? Didn't I care" (121)? Of course she cares very much; she loves Jay. But religiously, she cares very little. The telephone rings. "*God* help me, whispers Mary" (122). Ironically, the caller is her father. He offers comfort; he brings none, and Mary tells Hannah, "it's only Papa" (123). There is very little that any father can offer her now. Mary's internal struggle intensifies. The conversation turns to her father, who had opposed her marriage to Jay. She had, obviously, gone against his wishes. She asks Hannah: "It wasn't a mistake. Was it?" And Hannah, old, wise and long since having created a good distance between herself and God, thinks: "Don't ask me child, tell me" (125). Hannah senses Mary's newly discovered independence. She is pleased with Mary's questioning attitude and observes that her "soul is beginning to come of age" (125). In a most moving passage Agee writes, "Her heart lifted up in a kind of pride in Mary . . . She wanted to hold her niece at arms' length and to turn and admire this blossoming. She wanted to take her in her arms and groan unto God for what it meant to be alive" (127). And I add, particularly to be a woman. Hannah senses liberation, a groaning of a woman to free herself from some great travail, rather, hundreds of years of a male-dominated religious tradition that spoke for her but never to her.

Hannah now becomes her mentor. She urges Mary to accept what has happened as a beginning of a way of life and not an ending. For the first time, Mary can take charge of her life, do things, says Hannah, "by yourself . . . it's better if you learn it for yourself" (128). It will be hard because it is not easy to lose one's God. Mary's foundations, the father-god model, though masculine and false, are foundations nonetheless, and they have been snatched out from under her. She must begin to rebuild, and she feels the awesomeness of such a task. She laments, "I feel so utterly unprepared." But Hannah comforts her: "I don't think it's a kind of thing that can be prepared for; it just has to be lived through" (128). From her own experiences, Mary must create new models and new metaphors for God.

With new vigor, Mary's first response is to try and pray again. Bolstered by the presence of Hannah, she believes that she can complete her unfinished prayer. Hannah kneels with her but thinks, "God is not here" (129). Stiltedly they utter the Our Father. But Agee points out, "Something mistaken, unbearably piteous, infinitely malign was at large in that faithfulness; she was helpless to know its nature. Suddenly there opened with her a chasm of infinite depth and from it flowed the paralyzing breath of eternal darkness" (129).

The problem is, of course, that it is not enough to enter into a patriarchal world with only a new awareness. The religious myth of man has been written. There remains little written, at least in Western religion, about the religious myth of woman.[8] Hannah, the older and undoubtedly the more tired, chooses cynicism. She whispers, "I believe nothing." Yet Mary needs a religious myth, and she is like a child, anxiously ready, with no choice now but to grow personally and religiously. She retires to the bathroom, "humbled that one should obey such a call at such a time. She felt for a few moments as stupid and enslaved as a baby on its potty" (130). Her child-like attitude at having found something new--even in tragedy--is quite evident. Hannah expresses gratitude for our animal-like qualities.[9] The bestial nature--a return to a primal state suggests a return to a time before a patriarchal culture's influence. Mary can now experience new growth, religiously, free from certain restraints that were predicated on her relationship to Jay. There is something very natural about our inability to control, indefinitely, our bladders. There is something quite natural in Mary's new-found attitude about life and her place in it. Mary now says that she is ready to take control of her life. Hannah affirms that she is and then confronts God with her own prayer, "Here she is and she is adequate to the worst and she has done it for herself, not through my help or even, particularly through Yours. See to it that you appreciate her" (131).

Hannah is the stronger and can make claims in her wise and hardened old age that Mary cannot. While Mary has begun the process of change, the father-model of God is, unfortunately for her, still a part of her world-view. "I'm not going to say he's dead," she says, . . . "till I know he is . . . But I'm all but certain he is, all the same . . . I think what's very much more likely is that he was already dead when the man just phoned" (131). The father-god model, in a Yahwistic sense, was, is, will not be comforting to or instructive to women. More pernicious is that a God long since dead maintains such strong and oppressive influence over the lives of men and women.

Mary ends the chapter with a final prayer. "Oh I do beseech *my* God that it not be so" (132), perhaps a direct response to the opening prayer of Andrew's, "O my God," in response to the news about Jay. It is Mary's first attempt at affirming a personal God. The men now arrive with Jay's body. He is dead and so is the Father-God model. Mary, for the remainder of the novel, is inconsistent in her dealings with God, but her relationship with God is never the same as before. She exclaims towards the end of the text, "I am meeting it face to face, I am living through it" (286). Surely, the next step for Mary is to create her own God model, a new model that lends substance and nurture to her life.

Mary discovers that the God-the-Father model is inadequate and cannot meet her religious needs as woman. She has also discovered that she needs a personal God--the *my* of her prayer--a God that speaks to her experience as a woman. Mary seeks the God of *philia*, a God of familial friendship and love. She must look for a metaphor for God that illuminates her own experience. Sallie McFague would call this a "redescription" of reality.[10] While Mary's new found metaphor is not the reality itself, the reality of God, for Mary, is never gone, the metaphor is "a construct or interpretation" of reality.[11] And the metaphor or model should be selected because it makes sense out of Mary's experience.

Mary discovers the limited ability of masculine metaphors for God to give religious substance to her life. She now takes control of her life and interprets her own relationship with God. Mary creates her own metaphor. The most profound religious experience is found in the family matrix. Perhaps her new metaphor for God might be the one McFague calls "God as Friend."[12] Indeed, family, particularly Hannah, speaks personally to those most profound dimensions of Mary's experience. God is discovered and made real to Mary in those acts of *philia* that have their most authentic expression within the family setting.

IV

The theology of William James attempts to describe a way to live in the world both ontically and psychologically. The human creature is pragmatic and seeks simply to live a life personally productive and beneficial. He writes, "Not God, but life, more life, a larger, richer, more satisfying life, is, in the last analysis the end of religion."[13] Transcendence is wholly possible for James. Nonetheless, James wants the religious life acted out and rooted in the world. The happy and productive religious individual must find an "effective occupation of a place in life, with its dynamic currents passing through . . . being."[14] Religion for James provides an inworld reality that satisfies the emotional and psychological needs of the human creature. Father Jackson's advice to Mary on how to find comfort in her husband's death is useless; it has no utility. He offers transcendent, non-experiential reasons for the death and for how Mary should respond. Rather than focusing on Mary's needs, the priest offers theological dogma and structures. Neither James nor Agee is theocentric. The first question is not, "What does God desire?" The important question is, "What are the apparent needs of the human creature." Agee answers this question with the virtue *philia*.

James and Agee both argue for a religious view of the world that is relational. James argues on a level more symbolic and metaphorical, while Agee argues at a level quite literal. Both describe a need that persons have for something of ultimate value in their lives that informs all aspects of existence. James calls the value religion, "the feelings, acts, and experiences of individual men in their solitude, so far as they apprehend themselves to stand in relation to whatever they may consider the divine."[15] Agee calls the value the family. Most important, each argues for a "connectedness" in life that offers what James suggests is perhaps the most critical psychological characteristic of religion, "An assurance of safety and a temper of peace, and, in relation to others, a preponderance of loving affections."[16] We see this experience most vividly at the end of the text in the newly discovered relationship between Rufus and Andrew.

Persons are psychologically at home in the world only if persons have an in-world foundation on which to place hope and confidence. For James, religion is, even in its relation to "otherness," "the subconscious continuation of our conscious life."[17] The implications here suggest that we must be grounded in the world. The idea that religion must have a certain embeddedness in the world explains to some degree why Mary found the God-the-Father model useless in her religious crisis.

For Agee, the function of family is to ground us in the world. Family, acts of *philia*, becomes a model of religious expression. To be grounded in the world, within family, provides persons with the possibility of what James calls, "reaching unity; the process of remedying inner incompleteness and reducing inner discord."[18] The death of Jay Follet brings fragmentation to the members of the Follet family. Ralph sinks further into alcohol, Hannah into unbelief,

Andrew into agnosticism. But fragmentation is momentary when family members turn to one another. In acts of *philia*, they discover the strength to overcome their dissolution. Ralph becomes aware of his adolescent behavior. Hannah recovers spiritual strength in the process of helping Mary endure her tragedy. Andrew finds religious significance in the death of his brother, Jay. These persons discover unity in their personal lives because of their connectedness to family.

Facing finitude is perhaps the most anxious moment of any person's existence. When a family member dies, the anxiety is all the more real. James explains that persons need a connectedness to something that is "a stimulus, and excitement, a faith, a force that re-enforces the positive willingness to live, even in full presence of the evil perceptions that erewhile made life seen unbearable."[19] Mary is near hysteria at the thought of Jay's death. She tells Hannah that she and Jay had "come to a kind of harmoniousness" in their marriage. With young children still to raise, she sees no way to go on. Hannah offers moral support, prays with her, though she doesn't want to. Most important, Hannah is there through Mary's emotional and spiritual crisis.

The religious nature of familial connectedness is its enduring value. James suggests that one's religious conversion is to "the habitual centre of . . . personal energy,"--"the hot place."[20] The virtue that most informs personal existence, whether moral or religious, must be lasting. Agee emphasizes the enduring nature of family in the long, italicized story--the flashback--of his family's visit to the birthplace of the Follet family. The old woman, "almost as old as the country"(218), represents an encounter with origins of family. The moment of contact between the youngest of the clan, Rufus, and the oldest of the family, grandmaw, is marked by Rufus' unprompted and spontaneous kiss of the old woman, followed by her uncontrollable urination. Life waters give blessings to the reunion of family. The idea of family takes on a primordial, enduring connotation.

Indeed, the conclusion of Agee's novel is very similar to James' idea of "new birth." "New birth" is a "psychological form of event,--a firmness, stability, and equilibrium succeeding a period of storm and stress and inconsistency."[21] Agee's exaggerated conclusion to *A Death in the Family* uses the butterfly to symbolize new birth and resurrection at Jay's funeral. Yet the focus of the concluding paragraph is not Jay and the possibility of human resurrection; rather, the focus is Andrew's experience of new birth. Andrew is the family's agnostic member but discovers, in the life and death of his brother Jay, religious meaning founded on *philia*--his love for Jay. He is angry because the church refuses to read the complete service at Jay's funeral. Andrew believes that Jay's life was profoundly religious. He describes the episode of the butterfly as "surely miraculous" (314-5). So moved is Andrew that he must tell Rufus, who was not allowed to attend the funeral, all about the incident. Andrew turns to family to unencumber himself of his most perplexing problems.

James suggests that "religion thus makes easy and felicitous what in any case is necessary."[22] Family, for Agee, makes it possible for persons to endure, with differing degrees of happiness, what the world says "in any case is necessary." Family is the world's most religious dimension. *Philia* is the virtue that grounds existence and lends hope and possibility to the human endeavor. If one is to know the good life, Agee suggests that one must turn to familial love, the place of identity, nurture, and unremitting acceptance. Family provides a person with an inherent rootedness in the world and a way of "reaching unity . . . the process of remedying inner incompleteness and reducing inner discord." The good life is living the life of *philia*, a familial at-homeness in the world that provides religious and moral meaning for one's existence.

CHAPTER 3

"AND THERE IS NO HEALTH IN US"[1]:
WALKER PERCY'S *LOVE IN THE RUINS*

Walker Percy's writing reveals a people and a world spiritually diseased and unhealthy. The good news is that persons and worlds can change. The bad news is that they will not change in this life. Human beings lack the spiritual "stuff" that makes their lives meaningful and spiritually healthy. The world, no more than a reflection of the human creature's spiritual dearth, is mute to questions of ultimate value and meaning. Thus, the existential crisis in the lives of Percy's characters is how to cope with meaninglessness. A character's dis-ease with the world prompts the question, "Why?" Dis-ease implies at-ease. Unhealthiness implies healthiness. Percy's characters seek to complete the dialectic. If human beings are, as Percy suggests, exiles and wanderers in their own lands,[2] from what are they exiled and to what are they wandering?

Percy tells us that he writes from a world-view which is "incarnational, historical, and predicamental."[3] Religiously, human beings have gotten themselves into a spiritual "bog" from which they cannot extricate themselves, and, left alone, they will only get in deeper. The human predicament is the belief that, "I can make it on my own." Percy believes that history supports his view and that such a view has its best depiction in the Christian story of the Fall. The Christian answer to this predicament is the incarnation. We are exiled from God, and we are wandering in search of God. Only God can rescue us from our predicament.

Percy's is a pessimistic view of the world, *this* world, and in religious terms, Percy might be called a Manichaen. The human creature's origins represent a separation from the divine. The material world and the fleshy body represent evil captors of the divine spirit. Faithful persons seek and, at some point in history, are restored to, actually "saved-to" their divine origins. While Percy is not as extreme in his theology as the third century Manichaens; nonetheless, he suggests that the world is a diseased and fallen place which offers little, if any, religious sustenance. The world and other persons cannot be trusted to offer answers to questions about the nature, purpose, and intent of humanity.

Percy's religious world-view is transcendence. While human beings are estranged and alienated from any spiritual center, hope does remain for restoration. Yet hope is not found in the fragmented world of the human creature; rather, hope must be found in a transcendent world that is God's. Such hope requires the virtue faith. Faith does not change the world. The world's spiritual dis-ease is not so easily overcome. But faith does change the way an individual looks at the world. Persons recognize spiritual unhealthiness for what it is, a condition natural to the human creature. They recognize their need for something other than self and the world to give them spiritual health. That something, that critical virtue in Percy's religious world-view, is faith. Persons have faith in a transcendent whole, God, who brings hope to a world that is hopeless. Faith is the solution to the human crisis of spiritual meaninglessness.

In a world so afflicted by evil, acts of faith take on an apocalyptic tenor. Percy suggests that "we are living in eschatological times, times of enormous danger and commensurate hope, of possible end and possible renewal."[4] A faith commitment has catastrophic implications. Only through religious ordeal does a person come to himself and stand in judgment of his fallen state within a fallen world. Spiritual turmoil leads characters to religious conversion and to the discovery of faith. Such discovery represents an apocalypse of the soul. Persons have an extreme loss of confidence in the world's ability to reveal religious meaning and look elsewhere for spiritual direction and religious meaning for their lives. Religious ordeal that accompanies the spiritual quest leads to an encounter with "otherness," and requires an act of faith in a transcendent God.

Percy's novel, *Love in the Ruins*,[5] portrays the human being and the world that he/she lives in as spiritually diseased and unhealthy. Nothing short of catastrophic, personal conversion to theism, a transcendent God, can bring religious health and meaning to the life of the human creature. The dominant virtue discovered by Percy's character in quest for religious meaning is faith. Thomas More, the protagonist, must have faith in an "other" world, God's world, if his spiritual dis-ease is to be put at-ease.

I

Percy's description of spiritual disease falls into several categories without being contained within any one. He seems to be eclectic in the sources he draws upon to describe the spiritually unhealthy state of his protagonist in *Love in the Ruins*, Dr. Thomas More. Tom More suffers from Sartre's nausea, Freud's *thanatos* instinct, and/or Kierkegaard's sickness unto death, despair. In other words, Percy's character is irresponsible, not in control of his life, and a spiritual pilgrim estranged from any spiritual center. I will give a brief description of each "illness" and provide a substantive reference to what I believe Percy means when describing Thomas More as spiritually unhealthy. Of course, this list is incomplete. Because of Percy's existential bent, I could add Camus' absurdity, or even simply describe the anguish of Dostoyevsky's Raskolnikov.

Sartre suggests that the impasse between the mind's desire for explanation and the world's inability to give meaning creates nausea. When meaning is not so obvious in the world, the human creature attempts to force meaning on the world. As Roquentin explains in Sartre's classic text, *Nausea*, "you're always looking for something."[6] The inability to find "something," meaning, results in a sickening feeling of helplessness, says Roquentin, a "slipping into the water's depths, towards fear."[7]

As frightening as it may seem to live in a world that is meaningless, even more frightening is to know that one is alone in the world. Each person is, "forsaken in the present,"[8] lost in a world of contingencies he/she cannot escape. The human situation creates extreme irony. The world which is meaningless requires an imputation of meaning by the human creature. Roquentin discovers that he is the one "who unifies all sounds and shapes."[9] The human being finds the burden of meaning almost too weighty to bear; nonetheless, the burden is necessary and constant. The person who recognizes such grave responsibility begins to feel the knot in the stomach, the nausea that never leaves, or as Roquentin says, that "holds me."[10]

Roquentin's awareness of such radical responsibility is his victory, yet his is a hollow victory. He must impose meaning on a world that defies imposition. Roquentin can do little more than to feel sick at his fate. His newly discovered awareness tells him no more than he exists in a frighteningly unpredictable world. "I am free . . . I am alone . . . Alone and free. But this freedom is rather like death."[11]

Percy's character, Thomas More, experiences the same solitude in his spiritual quest for meaning. When meaning is not found in the world, he suffers Roquentin's nausea. More calls his illness "succubi, night exaltations, morning terror, and nameless longings" (181). Perhaps More's sickness is even *more* severe. He can find no relief in the freedom to make his own meaning; such efforts are futile. Yet unlike Roquentin, More does have faith. He relies on an "other" world, the world of a transcendent God, to bring health to his life. Nausea is not overcome; More must still live in the world. Like Roquentin, More is alone and free in the world, but he has more than the inchoate world to define his existence.

Spiritual illness leads to self-destruction. For Freud, the desire that drives us towards self-destruction is the death instinct. Freud tells us that "men are not gentle creatures who want to be loved . . . they are, on the contrary, creatures among whose instinctual endowments are to be reckoned a powerful share of aggressiveness."[12]   The death instinct explains societal as well as personal breakdown. Uncurtailed, the death instinct is violent, masochistic, and sadistic. Indeed, the death instinct has all the qualities of an illness and seeks pleasure at the expense of all ethical and moral considerations.

The human struggle becomes one between life and death. Freud says that "the meaning of the evolution of civilization is no longer obscure to us. It must present the struggle between Eros and Death, between the instinct of life and the instinct of destruction, as it works itself out in the human species."[13]   Without some outstanding authority requiring restraint over those natural desires towards self and societal destruction, human beings will not live the good life. According to Freud, the anxiety that holds society in a vice-like grip is the constant threat that the human instinct of aggression and destruction will "master" all efforts toward achieving the good and civilized life.

Society is decadent, aggressive, and fragmented in *Love in the Ruins*. We are reminded often that these are the last days. Thomas More has attempted suicide, lives on the mental ward of a hospital, and cannot control his self-destructive alcoholism. The human creature is a "self ripped from self" (360), revealing the instinctual struggle between the life and death instincts. Persons seek authority not only to bring meaning to existence, but also to keep life mentally balanced.

Thomas More's spiritual illness is original sin. The human creature, says Percy, has suffered from an "aboriginal catastrophe."[14] Freud's death instinct is what St. Paul describes as the urge to do "not . . . what I want," but "the very thing I hate."[15]   The authority, the superego, which holds sin in check is, for Percy, the transcendent God of Christian theism. The spiritual disease is original sin, the death instinct; the cure is faith in God, the civilized superego.

When Thomas More observes that the people around him are only going through the motions of living, while, in reality they are "dead," he could be echoing Kierkegaard. Persons who are spiritually unhealthy, in time, succumb to the "sickness unto death," despair. Immersed in the sensory life, which Kierkegaard calls the aesthetic life, a person is unsatisfied; life remains full of longings. The human life is a composite of opposite parts, finite and infinite, body and spirit, temporal and eternal. When a person lives only the sensual life, he/she fails to complete the dialectic, to give significant consideration to the spiritual dimensions of life.

Dread develops in the life of the human creature because he/she is spiritually unfulfilled and therefore unhealthy. He/She longs for completeness, for a wholeness that is inaccessible as long as he/she is living the life of sensory satisfaction, but the world is incapable of giving meaning to the human's spiritual longings. As long as the human creature attempts to find solution to spiritual crisis in the world, he/she will be a victim of the spiritual illness of despair.

Despair causes a person to feel a certain lostness and alienation in the world. By refusing to recognize spiritual identity, the human being loses all sense of personal identity. In *Repetition* Kierkegaard writes:

> One sticks a finger into the ground to smell what country one is in: I stick my finger into the world--it has no smell. Where am I? What does it mean to say: the world? What is the meaning of that word? Who tricked me into this whole thing and leaves me standing here? Who am I?[16]

Spiritual illness results in lack of place and identity. Persons become religious pilgrims and sojourners seeking meaning and purpose for their lives. Purpose comes only by an act of faith, a renunciation of this world's ability to give ultimate meaning to human existence. The act of faith brings God to bear on the spiritual component of human existence, a component innate but of which one is unaware until the act of faith.

Thomas More suffers from the spiritual sickness of despair. Embedded for the most of his life in the world of sensual gratification, he seeks meaning in the world. The keys to life are sexuality and technology. But each fails to satisfy his innate spiritual nature. He finds himself alienated and dislocated in a world void of religious sustenance. He is homeless and becomes a sojourner, a religious pilgrim. More's religious quest is to complete the dialectic of the temporal and eternal or to find, he says, the "dosage to weld the broken self whole" (35). He is made whole only through an act of faith in which he renounces the things of this world and their abilities to make him religiously healthy and places total trust in the transcendent God's commitment to creation. Faith, for Percy, is a person's admission, if not confession, that he/she cannot live the good life without help from God.

II

Plot is the narrative element critical to the fullest appreciation of character in Percy's novel, *Love in the Ruins*. The plot provides a framework for understanding characters' "crises of the soul," and plot is the narrative element that best reveals the apocalyptic nature of the text. The plot of a text, by function, is well suited for apocalyptic interpretation. A plot establishes time, breaks time, and almost always restores time by bringing a text to its *denouement*.

The idea of apocalypse is closely related to the narrative element plot because each is intimately related to time. Time in apocalypse is fragmented by religious crisis and is brought to a moral or religious wholeness. Time in a plot is the process of "sorting-out" a life usually beset by crisis. Through ritual and repetition, plot brings character to a discovery of a solution that best "sorts-out" his/her life.

The plot of Percy's text is apocalyptic and establishes character within a time of spiritual crisis. Therefore, the plot of the text is important in revealing the spiritually unhealthy nature of the human creature. In fact, the spiritual crisis of character is the disease of meaninglessness. As plot moves character through a pilgrimage towards meaning, the plot reveals its apocalyptic and crisis-oriented tendencies.

The apocalyptic nature of *Love in the Ruins* and the manner in which the plot line reveals the text's crisis-orientation are revealed by a close look at Percy's use of music as apocalyptic symbol in the text. Music, which has an innate sense of plot and apocalypse, is used as an interpretive text *within* Percy's text. The creative language of music is powerfully apocalyptic: *diminuendo, adagio, poco a poco retard, allegretto, fortissimo*. Percy uses the plot and apocalyptic overtones of Mozart's opera *Don Giovanni* to intensify and emphasize the apocalyptic nature of *Love in the Ruins*. The use of a plot within a plot, while confusing, is symbolic not only of the complicated and complex nature of human existence, but also of the fragmented and brokenness of time in life's apocalyptic and dis-eased orientation within the world. The threat of moral judgment and the personal experience of spiritual crisis connect Percy's novel and Mozart's opera in terms of plot and apocalypse. Apocalypse, ultimately, is the relationship between time and eternity. For Percy, apocalypse suggests a way to look forward to immanent ends in a manner that informs, structures, and gives meaning to the whole of life. Thus, apocalypse is a form of plotting. Spiritual crisis reaches catastrophic proportions when it makes a person ask, "How do I live in the world, with meaning and purpose, knowing that I am going to die." Finitude is the ultimate threat to meaning and certainly is plot's most threatening *denouement*.

The novel's central character, Thomas More, is never happier than those moments alone, in his office, listening to *Don Giovanni*.[17] When he is not listening to Mozart's opera, he is humming particular arias or duets to himself. Don Giovanni and Thomas More are the same characters. More suffers from morning terrors and hives--spiritual diseases which cause a certain disorientation in his relation to the world- -and compensates for his dis-ease with life through immersion in immediate pleasures: Early Times whiskey, his lapsometer, and women. Giovanni, too, is consumed by the present. His life is one of banquets and sexual conquests. More has three women, all three of whom attract him sexually, waiting for him in an abandoned Howard Johnson's. Giovanni has 1003 conquests in Spain alone. Women are objects he uses to distraction in order to avoid the weightier problems of life. More loves women best, and so does Giovanni. Giovanni's servant describes him: "Ill or healthy, Poor or wealthy, Plain or pretty, Dull or witty, High-born, lowly, scraggly hags or beauties, Be they female, they're his duties" (48). Absorption with the sex act frees both More and Giovanni from dwelling on their feelings of dislocation in the world. Giovanni, only a few moments after killing the father of a lover, exclaims, "that scent is, surely, feminine" (31), and begins the hunt anew for sexual pleasures.

Opera and literary text both have strong components of moralism. For Percy, one endures this world and is patient while trying to follow the golden rule, aware all along that, at best, the golden rule is an ideal of the heart and that one lives in the world a tragic hero. The Rotary Banner at the Howard Johnson's reads, "Is it the truth? Is it fair to all concerned? Will it build goodwill and better friendship?" But the banner is "rent top to bottom" (9). One can only grope for a sense of place in light of God's plans for all eternity and wait for the imminent, final hour, when God will vindicate the good.

Moralism plays an even more explicit role in *Don Giovanni*. The message is clear; doom awaits those who do not repent of their sins. God's vengeance is quick and sure. God dispatches Giovanni "to enter the undying fire" where his "bowels melt in agony" (281) because he refuses to repent for the murder of his lover's father. "Kneel, pray to God for pardon,!" he is told. He answers, no, "I scorn him, I defy him" (278). For Mozart and his librettist, Lorenzo Da Ponte, morality is inextricably bound to judgment. This view is not unlike Percy's. For both there remains a strong sense of ironic optimism that imminent judgment awaits the wicked and vindication awaits those who are enduringly just and contrite of heart. Therefore, we "sing the old song again," says Mozart. "So do all deceivers end, deceivers end, So they end . . . Rakes, betrayers, all take warning, while there's time still your ways to mend . . . So mend your way" (292).

A close look at the Overture with references to Acts I and II reveals that the score of the opera, like the novel, unfolds apocalyptically; in fact, the opera is quite intricately plotted. The opera is Mozart's first in which the Overture begins slowly, *andante*. The *andante* creates a sense of awe and prescience and prepares the listener for the demise of Giovanni and his deceitful adventures. Tension mounts and anticipation heightens. Percy's novel begins with the "latter days;" more exact, Thomas More explains, "two more hours should tell the story . . . catastrophe will occur" (3). Having prepared us for the cataclysmic end in the first chapter, he then, in the remaining text, recalls the three days leading up to the final day. Mozart's Overture and Percy's first chapter take us immediately to the apex of each work's apocalyptic moment.

Mozart then moves brightly into the *allegro*. The *allegro* is character description. The music is original and disoriented, and is found, surprisingly, nowhere else in the opera. Some parts suggest pomposity; other parts suggest melancholia. Transitions are swift, and rhythms are pulsating. The music is descriptive of Giovanni. He, too, is pompous, sprightly, and disoriented. He is, also, hot blooded and quick-witted. But he lacks sustained substance. He is the only main character in the opera who has no long aria. One critic suggests that no character in opera has such significant stage time yet demonstrates such vacuity. Thomas More is no different. Until the end of the novel, he has no sense of place and no spiritual depth. He describes his life as full of "nameless longings" and plagued by "morning terror" (181).

Mozart's attempt to ally the Overture with the action of the opera is successful. This first movement foreshadows the moment in the Second Act's finale, the opera's most apocalyptic moment, when a ghostly statue of the murdered lover's father warns Giovanni to repent of his sins or suffer severe consequences. Musically, this moment looms large in the Overture. The statue enters Giovanni's banquet room with a powerful burst of pure D minor, a blast that is "pregnant with dramatic menace".[18] We know that this is the same moment in the second act; we simply need the statue's lyrics to complete the piece. The trombones are missing from the Overture; Mozart saves their eerie and mystical power for the finale. But we are prepared, in the Overture, for Giovanni's descent into hell. "Anguished scales ascend *crescendo* "[19] as God's messenger confronts the rogue and demands repentance. Oboes strain, almost wail; "wan" flutes slide fluidly along scales. But then follows hesitation, and an E flat chord solemnly brings the banquet scene and Giovanni's judgment to a climax.

Thomas More has his own "descent into hell" (156). Peering "through the smoke" (355) at his messenger from God, a Jobian tempter by the name of Art Immelman, More is given a choice between the escapism of his old life or a new life of expectancy and fidelity. But the good doctor does not, like Giovanni, curse or defy God; instead, he beseeches his patron saint. "Sir Thomas More, kinsman, saint, but dearest, merriest of Englishmen, pray for us and drive this son of a bitch hence" (355). His prayer is answered. More's stone figure is banished.

Mozart's opera ends with a double fugue that has a certain kinship with the sacred music of his time. Giovanni, immune to human justice, receives his just desserts from God. The righteous, now vindicated, go on about their lives. And Thomas More? He no longer listens to *Don Giovanni* but barbecues in his "sack cloth" and sips Early Times whiskey while the *Salve Regina* plays on the stereo (378).

The plot in each story brings character to completion. For Giovanni, the end is death, and for More, the end is a conversion to faith in God. Each character undergoes a personal apocalypse that is highlighted by plot. Each character has a spiritual crisis that is brought to a solution. Percy chooses to place the apocalyptic *Don Giovanni* within *Love in the Ruins* to emphasize the text's apocalyptic plot and the catastrophic nature implicit in the act of faith.

III

The process of character development and discovery in *Love in the Ruins* unfolds in three stages. First, the text establishes the spiritually unhealthy nature of the novel's central character, Thomas More. For emphasis, More's spiritually diseased life is reflected in the decadent and fragmented physical world in which he lives. Second, character moves towards transcendence--a faith relationship with an "other"--when he is unable to achieve spiritual health on his own. The character's attempts to make meaning for his life, without God, either through dependence on technology--a mental abstraction--or through pleasures of the flesh--a bestial immersion into the world--fail. Third, a character "comes to himself," a spiritual awareness of his need for a transcendent God. At this point, for Percy, a Christian scheme takes over. A character is contrite, confesses his sins, and has faith in God. The act of faith does little to change the world but radically changes the character who lives in the world.

The world in which Thomas More lives is literally fragmented and broken. The language illustrates the physical and moral decay of the times. More explains that "these are bad times" (5) we live in. Abandoned shopping centers and motels are commonplace. Streets and sidewalks are cracked and sprouting vines. Cars are driven until they break down and, then, are abandoned. The problem, says More, is that "things stopped working and nobody wanted to be a repairman" (60). His assertion, he soon discovers, is theological. The human creature is incapable of self-repair. Only the person who can have "contrition and a firm purpose of amendment" (374) can live in a world which is by nature decayed. Even the church to which More belongs is literally fragmented and broken, spiritually unhealthy. The Catholic Church is "split into three pieces: 1. the American Catholic Church whose new Rome is Cicero, Illinois; 2. the Dutch schismatics who believe in relevance but not God; 3. the Roman Catholic remnant, a tiny scattered flock with no place to go" (5). Indeed, the true remnant has no place to go in this world. "For the world," says More, "is broken, sundered, busted down the middle, self ripped from self and man pasted back together as mythical monster, half angel, half beast, but no man" (360). The problem is existential. The human creature is alone, tottering between terror and hope and attempting to find a center--religious meaning--that will "hold" (18).

Yet society's physical and moral decay serves merely to mirror the deeper, more profound spiritual decay and chaos in the soul of the individual, particularly Tom More. The story begins with More sitting against a diseased tree, a pine with a "tumor." The diseased tree merely reflects the spiritually unhealthy More. The play on the name is appropriate; religiously, he needs *more*. He sits against the tree and looks out over the "interstates," awaiting catastrophe. Yet catastrophe will not come down the interstate highway, but must happen to the "inner" state of More's religious condition. A solution to More's religious crisis will not come from outside, in a world fallen and meaningless, but only from inside, a spiritual rebirth within the important "inner" state.

This spiritual condition is common to all persons. Father Smith, More's priest and certainly the most spiritually insightful person in the text, has been driven insane by the world's lack of contrition and a people's paucity of faith. He tells More: "Death is winning, life is losing." To which the physician responds: "The living? Do you mean the living are dead? Yes," says Smith, "I mean their souls of course. . . I am surrounded by the corpses of souls. We live in a city of the dead" (176-7).

More is everyman. He is, in terms of Christian orthodoxy, a fallen creature. He suffers from "hives" and "morning terror," Percy's terms for Roquentin's nausea. More is not "well" (106). He is a doctor who cures and a patient who is in need of a cure. At the hospital he is described as "patient-staff" (106) and has spent time in the acute wing of the psychiatric hospital after attempting suicide. Percy appears convinced that persons are at home with the sick. More describes himself with one sentence. "I believe in God and the whole business, but I love women best, music and science next, whiskey next, God fourth, and my fellowman hardly at all" (6). Most important, More's life is meaningless.

The result of More's spiritual illness, life's meaninglessness, is *ennui*, boredom. His life has no direction or purpose and an extreme resignation to time takes over his existence. More's boredom is objectless, like Kierkegaard's anxiety. He doesn't know why he suffers from a restlessness with life, and his unknowing makes life all the more frightening. More's condition, his spiritual malaise, is described in terms of sickness. Notice the passive voice of his suffering. He is "assaulted by succubi, night exaltations, morning terror, and nameless longings" (181). More's *ennui* and restlessness represent estrangement from God. Saint Augustine says: "My heart is restless until it finds rest in Thee." According to Percy, More is a spiritual "castaway, who despite a lifetime of striving to be at home . . . is as homeless now as he was the first day he found himself cast up on the beach."

Percy's description of More is consistent with the author's own theological understanding of Jewish and Christian history. W. L. Godshalk points out that we should interpret *Love in the Ruins* not as a "new vision of things but as a relatively old vision of the human condition."[20] Persons are religiously fallen and suffer from original sin. Percy explains that "the perennial estrangement of man" is part of the human condition, and the "cultural estrangement of Western man in the Twentieth century" is an "undeniable fact."[21] The Jewish and Christian traditions, suggests Percy, are the only traditions that hold firm to and believe in the "enduring symptom of man's estrangement from God."[22] Percy writes:

> It was the belief that man was created in the image of God with an immortal soul, that he occupied a place in nature somewhere between the beasts and the angels, that he suffered an aboriginal catastrophe, the Fall, in consequence of which he lost his way and, unlike the beasts, became capable of sin and thereafter became a pilgrim or seeker of his own salvation.[23]

More's spiritual disease makes him restless. He seeks something that will give meaning to his existence. What More discovers is that he cannot make meaning in a world spiritually empty and that he will need to depend on something "other" than this world or himself. Yet for the moment he immerses himself deeper into the world to find religious health and meaning.

More first seeks meaning in abstraction, the world of the mind and human technology. He is committed to the power and possibility of human reason to answer the most perplexing questions of human existence. He develops the lapsometer, a machine designed to gauge levels of beastialism and angelism, conditions of the human soul. The lapsometer is a product of the objective, scientific mind. Its function is to locate "the deep perturbations of the soul" (28). Yet this discovery is not a cure and simply reveals what was known before the machine's invention: "No sir, I'm not well" (194). The physician cannot cure the soul; such healing is found only along the "Sacred Way," faith in the transcendent God (181). More's new found technology can diagnose the human situation, but long after the diagnostic act, "night exaltations, morning terror, and nameless longings," still remain. The scientist can "observe, measure, verify," the sundered self, but only the forgiveness that accompanies faith can bridge "the dread chasm that has rent the soul of Western man ever since the famous philosopher

Descartes ripped body loose from mind and turned the very soul into a ghost that haunts its own house" (181).

Abstraction having failed, More turns to the human creature's more bestial nature to discover meaning. He seeks total immersion into the "things" of the world. The goal of the bestial nature is to "condition away the contradiction." If one abandons oneself to his/her basic instincts, More explains, "you'd never feel guilt" (112). More chooses late night sex in the bunker of the eighteenth hole with Lola, a cellist, who hisses Dvorak while making love. The encounter is sensuous, but the result is momentary, physical satisfaction. The fact that the act takes place in a bunker, not the green, is telling. The bunker is the "diseased" spot on the golf course.

Percy's most literal portrayal of the human creature's bestial nature is the love clinic. Sexuality is reduced to mechanism and habit. Participants in the clinics are no more than animals. In the love clinic, human relationship is measured by the intensity of orgasm. The oxymoronic name given to the institution is appropriate. The place is sterile and is perhaps the most love-barren place of all. Lillian is the love clinic's prize pupil. She comes to the laboratory where, "clipping Lucite fittings to sensor wires . . . she inserts one after another into the body orifices, as handily and thriftily as a teenager popping in a contact lens" (118). She begins "autostimulation;" a "vaginal computer" measures orgasm. Her act is meaningless and lonely. The irony is that she makes love in solitude, the very place in which there can be no love. And the people who operate the love clinic are as sterile and unemotional as the act they observe and measure. Father Ken Kevin was a curate but is now "chaplain of the clinic" and counsels persons "who cannot love," inversely a commentary on himself. Hulga Heine, a nurse, operates her job with "brick solemnity" (119), struggling to suppress her own sexual excitement as she watches volunteers engage in sex--a rather sad sort of voyeurism.

A world so void of meaning and so clinical in purpose serves only to frustrate More in his quest for spiritual health and meaning. He must look beyond machines of his own creation and the urgings of his groin to find answers to life's perplexing questions of identity and place in the world. The lapsometer and sex in the bunker of the eighteenth hole are, ultimately, mute to the critical questions of existence. Yet at this point we discover that fallenness represents the good news of Christianity. Secularism, says G. K. Chesterton, declares the world sick but without cure; Christianity recognizes the very same illnesses but suggests that a cure is at hand.

More finds a cure for his spiritual disease in a radical faith commitment to God. A life of question begins to discover answers when More turns to confession and sacrament and is willing "to feast on death," that is, eat Christ and give conscious assent to the incarnation. Conscious assent to the Christ event is an act of faith by which More says: "I cannot make it alone." He turns to an "other"-- the transcendent God--to bring meaning, purpose, and spiritual health to a life he describes as one of "drunkenness, lusts, envies, fornication, delight in the misfortunes of others, and loving myself better than God and other men" (374-5). The confession is his earlier self-description reversed. A spiritual condition that once confessed to love "women best, music and science next, whiskey next, God fourth, and my fellowman hardly at all" (6) has experienced a total conversion.

The setting of the final chapter is Christmas Eve, five years later. More is, essentially, awaiting the birth of the Christ child into his own life. The incarnation is that moment when eternity is brought to bear on the present. It is the act of a transcendent God that says that the world and those who people it matter. More says, you "eat Christ, drink his blood" (377), and; then, you "watch and listen and wait"(359). One makes a faith commitment to a transcendent "other," at which point, one lives in expectation and anticipates that one's God will act. More has learned to cope with the "principalities and powers" (176) of the world. He becomes truly contrite and says, "I'm sorry" for a life of misdeeds. More is "scalded" by his confession to his priest (376), a simple act of faith in which he submits himself to a power other than his own.

Do things change? More says: "I can't say things have changed much. What has changed is my way of dealing with it" (362). The world does not change. Faith brings new perspective to a fallen world and, most of all, an ability to live with self as a limited and spiritually diseased creature. More now marries his faithful nurse, Ellen. She is the "dour young and beautiful . . . Presbyterian who doesn't have much use for God but believes in doing right and does it" (361). They live outside the highly respectable "Paradise Estates." He and his wife live in the slave quarters. No longer, though, is More a slave to the world; he is a slave to his newly found faith in Christ. More must walk "up the cliff" to catch the bus in Paradise, a clear suggestion that life in the fallen world is more like purgatory than paradise. He moonlights at "a fat clinic" (365). The world remains broken and "in need of a repairman." In a small way, More, with his fat clinic, has become one.

More has a more realistic view of the world and his place in it. Gerald Kennedy suggests that he has learned "how to reconcile mind and body and recapture a sense of authenticity and wholeness about one's individual existence."[24] Ironically, he can assert his sovereignty because he has surrendered it to something greater than himself and to the expectation that he can change his life from a boring undirected existence to a life of meaning and direction. "Strange," he says, "I am older, yet there seems to be more time, time for watching and waiting and thinking and working. All any man needs is time and desire and the sense of his own sovereignty" (360). The "watching and waiting and thinking and working" are acts of submission, acts of faith that God, not the individual, is in control.

Of course, More's conversion is a bit anticlimactic. The Christian faith, explains Percy, is terribly unexciting. Christianity is "like a man who finds a treasure in his field and sells all he has to buy the field, only to discover that everyone else has the same treasure in his field and that in any case real estate values have gone so high that all field owners have forgotten the treasure and plan to subdivide."[25] But Thomas More's health, physical and spiritual, is better. He has "fewer shakes and depressions" (360). The physician is, to the degree that anyone can be, spiritually healed. He has had a baptism; "water is the mystical element" (360), he says while fishing in the early morning. The world has not changed; it remains "busted down the middle, self ripped from self" (360). But one can live in expectation, "waiting and watching," "eating Christ" aware that one's life balances at the brink of eternity.

IV

Love in the Ruins suggests that the virtue faith allows a person to live at peace with a world spiritually fragmented, unhealthy, and alien to the will of God. Persons of faith, while in this world, seem not to belong to this world; rather, persons of faith are pilgrims and sojourners. They are people of the spirit who seek the truth of God and set themselves over against the people of the flesh, people who are self-centered and prideful and who belong, too much to this world. People of faith inhabit "another world," while living in the present world. Faith promises, if we "watch and wait," that a time will come when God will bring a oneness to the fragmented world and when persons of faith will be united into a transcendent whole. Creation is an act of plotting; God has an end in mind for those who have faith.

Saint Augustine's classic text, *City of God*, gives a traditional, theological description of Walker Percy's religious world-view of transcendence. Augustine's theological categories of the two cities, one of God and the other of man, are very helpful in understanding Percy's novel *Love in the Ruins*. Percy appears very Augustinian in his belief that a person must live in the world but not be of the world and that the virtue faith allows for such a spiritual existence.

Faith completes the spiritual side of the dialectic that is at work in the lives of each human being. A person has a temporal side and a spiritual side. He/She may satisfy his/her temporal longings and desires within the world of material things and pleasures, but a person may satisfy his/her spiritual side only through a faith relationship with God. Augustine says that we are "created to the image of a Creator, whose eternity is true" and that "we contemplate His image in our very selves."[26] We are of the temporal and fallen world, but we seek the wholeness that comes with our return to the image of God. We seek what Augustine calls the "City of God."[27] We "long to become its citizens" because in the City of God we are closer to our natural state, the image of God. The act of faith makes us citizens of the City of God and makes whole the dialectic of the temporal and spiritual selves. Until we act in faith, we satisfy only our temporal longings and remain spiritually unhealthy, living in the city of men, and are condemned to an aimless quest for spiritual health.

Thus Thomas More is restless with "hives," "shakes," and "longings." He is immersed in the city of men. The city of men is the world of pride and falsehood.[28] In the earthly city, says Augustine, people "prefer their own gods to the founder of the Holy City."[29] More turns to technology, the lapsometer, to solve the spiritual problems of the age. Yet the machine is only diagnostic and can offer no cure. He turns to sensual pleasure, what Augustine calls one of the "four ends" to human nature.[30] More's god becomes the flesh. He seeks spiritual fulfillment in sexual relationship. His encounters are brief and their spiritual sustenance fleeting if not nonexistent. The earthly city "does not live by faith"[31], says Augustine. Meaningful existence is found in what he calls "the voluntary and collective attainment of objectives necessary to mortal existence."[32] This belief reveals the most common sin of the earthly city, *hubris*; we think that the earth is eternal. But if persons are to have spiritual health and wholeness, they must look beyond the city of men.

The City of God is "wayfaring on earth."[33] Faith in the will and purpose of God allows one to live as a faithful pilgrim in God's city.

Both the City of God and the city of men seek to order the world for healthy and peaceful existence. But the "City of God subordinates this earthly peace to that of heaven."[34] While the earthly city places faith in its own finite and limited creations, persons of the City of God place faith in the vision of "the world to come."[35] Persons of faith live with implicit trust in and in total capitulation to the will of God. Augustine points out that "when God commands, man obeys; when the soul commands, the body obeys; when reason rules, our passions, even when they fight back, must be conquered or resisted."[36]

Thomas More moves from faithless and aimless wanderer in the earthly city to faithful sojourner in the City of God. He lives at peace in the world but is not of the world. Augustine explains that "faith can assure our exodus from Babylon, but our pilgrim status, for the time being, makes us neighbors."[37] More now "watches, listens, and waits" in faith, for the City of God to be brought to fullness in time and to union with the heavenly city. He has faith that God has plotted a purpose and an end for the City of God or, according to Augustine, "that part that is on pilgrimage in mortal life and lives by faith."[38] More, like Augustine, believes that the City of God has an "appointed end." While there is no hope for spiritual change or health in the earthly city, people of faith expect God to make the City of God, on earth, one with the heavenly city. "Heaven . . . will be the fulfillment of that Sabbath rest foretold in the command: 'Be still and see that I am God.'"[39] More can now "work and wait" (361) for this event. He will still be tempted by the pleasures of the earthly city; he claims that he continues to believe that "the lapsometer can save the world--if I can get it right" (360). More will not be spiritually whole until God unites the pilgrims of the City of God on earth with the heavenly city. To be human is to be spiritually fragmented. Yet through faith More has learned to orchestrate the fragments of a life longing to "find rest" in God and that now follows the "Sacred Way." Having left the one city that, according to Augustine, "had its beginnings in the love of self," More now lives in the "humble City . . . of holy men and good angels . . . the one city began with the love of God."[40]

CHAPTER 4

THE LAND OF THE BRAVE:
ROBERT PENN WARREN'S *A PLACE TO COME TO*

Robert Penn Warren's religious category for understanding the world is tragedy. Tragedy is a result of human limitations. Characters in Warren's fiction are limited by space and time. Place of birth represents a person's spatial limitation because personal identity is intricately and intimately connected to and limited by the circumstances of one's birthplace and family. Human finitude is the limiting nature of time because the defining characteristic of being human is being mortal. In order to live a meaningful existence, a character in Warren's fiction must accept his limitations of space and time and the tragic circumstances that can result from such limitations.

In a tragic world, a character faces and accepts his limitations through acts of courage. A person takes responsibility for being in the world and lives "in spite of" the tragic events of human existence and the limitations on being human. Complicity with the world and the human community, with its tragic dimension, is the first step towards self-identity and is the "courage to be" in a world over which one has little control.[1] Such courage, says Dorothea Krook, is "pre-eminently moral: not a quality of mind but of character; not the courage or heroism of the contemplative spirit . . . but that of the man or woman immersed in life and living; therefore, a courage practical, applied, active, characteristically expressing itself in immediate responses to concrete moral situations."[2]

Self-identity, the goal of Warren's characters, is forged out of tragic circumstance and in response to human limitations. Faced with a religious dilemma, an existential crisis of personal liberty, a character makes a decision and has little if no control over its consequences. The character courageously accepts the consequences of his decision and forfeits freedom for stoic endurance. Warren's characters live in "the land of the brave." A character asks no questions about the best of all possible worlds; he simply endures the world he has. With stoic courage he accepts his lot in life.

The character Jed Tewksbury, in Robert Penn Warren's *A Place to Come To*,[3] discovers self-identity in life's tragic dimension. Faced with the human limitations of place and finitude, his existential crisis, Jed must choose to live courageously, aware and accepting of his limitations. Jed discovers the good news; the tragic dimension of life not only reveals human limitations but also provides opportunity for courageous living in confrontation with human limitations. Tragedy can reveal what is noble about being human. Thus courage is the virtue revealed by Warren's narrative and is the solution to his character's existential crisis. When Jed chooses courage to confront life's unpredictability and profoundly tragic dimension, his life reveals not only a true sense of self-awareness but also a tragic yet noble sense of stoic endurance. Jed, a courageous character who acts responsibly in a world of moral and religious dilemma, gains self-knowledge.

I

Warren is often called a Christian writer.[4] The claim is incorrect. Critics often use Christian language to describe the themes found in Warren's work: original sin, redemption, grace, reconciliation. He is often cited as an articulate interpreter of the Christian doctrine of original sin. Warren does suggest rather strongly that persons are inclined to evil. He distrusts Enlightenment thought which suggests a presumptuously overconfident and optimistic view of the self.[5] He holds at fault Emerson and the entire transcendentalist movement for an enduring and pervasive sense of optimism about human nature and American society.

Warren has written a poem of epic proportions, *Brother to Dragons*,[6] as an indictment of a positive view of human nature that suggests that people are good and reasonable and that common courtesy will one day triumph in a world of evil. The poem has an historical setting. Thomas Jefferson's nephews kill and butcher a slave who has dropped and broken a vase belonging to their mother. Jefferson, dead for some years, makes a ghostly visit to the scene of the crime. He is horrified that his own flesh and blood could commit such a heinous crime. The poem has a tremendous moral force, and persuades Jefferson to accept a dimmer view of the nature and possibility of the human creature. Lucy, Jefferson's sister, speaks the poem's philosophical conclusion, a rather cold realism that is tempered somewhat by unattainable possibilities.

> Your dream, my dear Brother, was noble. I'd not deny
> that. If there was vanity, fear, and deceit, in its

condition, what of that? For we are human, and must
work in the shade of our human condition. The dream
remains, but my dear Brother, if your dream was noble,
there's a nobler yet to dream. It will be nobler because
more difficult and cold in the face of the old cost of the
human redemption, and knowledge of that cost is, in
itself, a kind of redemption.[7]

Lucy suggests the courage to know oneself.

Warren's view of human nature is decidedly Puritan, and he has a
very real sense of moral evil. But his views are not Christian. He says
of himself: "I'm a yearner. I mean I wish I were religious . . . religion
is a necessary myth."[8] He goes on to say, about his novels, that they
are "about the quest for religion."[9] I suggest that Warren describes
Stoicism, not Christianity. He is religious but not Christian. He is
far more concerned with moral decision than with redemption, with self-
knowledge than with grace.

Most appealing to Warren would be Stoicism's insistence on the
value of the human individual in a world of discord. Paul Tillich
suggests that Stoicism is the "only real alternative to Christianity in
the Western world."[10] Warren's central characters have the Stoic
courage to live in a world tragic and indecipherable because they have
the courage to die. The Stoic accepts the human limitation of finitude--
the world of death--and, in turn, can immerse him/herself with a noble
vigor into a world of life. The Stoic rationally assumes the
unpredictable nature of existence then asserts a rational and courageous
attitude by which he/she confronts and endures the irrational world. The
Stoic finds courage at the extremes of existence. David Tracy calls such
extremes "limit-situations," a notion similar to what Karl Jaspers calls
"boundary-situations." As Tracy points out, "fundamentally the
concept refers to those human situations wherein a human being
ineluctably finds manifest a certain ultimate limit or horizon to his or
her existence."[11]

Jed Tewksbury, Warren's central character in *A Place to Come To*,
faces the tragic dimensions of his life with Stoic courage and
responsibility. His religious decision-making is not candy-coated by a
pie-in-the-sky attitude of forgiveness and ultimate salvation. On the
contrary, he is totally responsible for his choices and makes the most of
these choices without hope of a *deus ex machina* intervening. Peter
Stitt points out that "there is no point in promising man redemption if
you have to deny human nature to deliver; Warren is a realist, not a
dreamer; he justifies the promises he makes by admitting the truth of

what we are."[12] I suggest that implicit in Warren's fiction is the idea that there can be no Christian tragedy. Christianity ultimately relieves a person of responsibility for moral decision-making because one is ultimately forgiven.

II

The narrative element atmosphere in Warren's novel is essential to his depiction of the tragic life. Atmosphere establishes boundaries and limits for character, plot, and tone. Giles Gunn calls these limits "the hypothetical world" of the novel.[13] The author controls atmosphere by placing his/her story under certain restrictions.[14] Wesley Kort puts it succinctly, "because of atmosphere, narratives raise and answer the question of what is possible."[15] For this reason, the atmosphere of the text plays an important role in tragic literature. Tragedy reveals a respect for and the imposition of limits and boundaries. A character's limitations bring about his/her tragic demise. In tragedy, awareness of and belief in established boundaries are critical to a character's development. Atmosphere gives insight to tragedy's religious dimension because, like tragedy, atmosphere entreats belief in a religious system of "oughts" which are appropriate and necessary for the good life.

Warren, in *A Place to Come To*, establishes obvious boundaries for his characters. These boundaries are space and time. Characters are brought to religious decision in response to their limitations. Jed explains that one tries "to live in a new medium, in which there was [is] no past and no future, only the strange present," but inevitably the "old weight-clock in the hall" ticks (189). All religious decisions are a consequence of this connection to the human family--place, and a universal nature--finitude. These decisions affect the self-awareness of the individual. Self-identity is discovered by accepting a common bond with all of humanity. A person recognizes "place" and "nature" in the human family by first recognizing his/her relation to an immediate family. The narrative element of atmosphere reveals what is possible for a character in confrontation with life's tragic dimension. Because atmosphere and tragedy emphasize human limitations, personal freedom is not an issue in tragic existence. Jed is free to respond to his human limitations but is not free to reject them.

Yet tragedy is more than narrative atmosphere. Tragedy has its origins in both the individual and the social order.[16] The tragic hero, experiences a demise for two inextricably related reasons. First, he chooses evil out of ignorance of self and because of human limitation.

Faced with multiple decisions in a lifetime, he will at some point make a bad decision. Second, there exists, inherent in the social order, a natural law, a world order that cannot be violated or it brings about human downfall. A person is responsible only to the degree that he recognizes that he is a part of the human family that suffers, *in toto*, from the imposition of a natural order, which must remain inviolate. While a person is not responsible for the natural/moral order, a person is responsible for recognizing and accepting it. Jed Tewksbury's life attains tragic proportions when he attempts to confront and overcome the human limitations of place and finitude.

III

Jed refuses to accept the human limitation of place. His life is a constant attempt to deny place of origin and its informative influence on his life. But place of birth is perhaps one of the most informative and powerful influences on human existence and self-definition. And the limiting nature of place is only magnified when one tries to deny or escape it. Jed's unwillingness to accept his place of birth takes on tragic dimensions and thwarts all his efforts at self-identity. Particular events during three critical stages in Jed's life reveal his attempts to escape all ties to his place of birth. These attempts are made during the periods of Jed's childhood, his formal education, and his professional life.

Jed is born in Claxford County, Dugton, Alabama. The area is economically depressed, socially limited, and intellectually stagnant. He is encouraged by his mother to escape the area. She tells him, "Do you know how it come to be?" . . . One time there was a pigeon big as the Rocky Mountain and he had stuffed his-self on all the pokeberries and cow patties this side of Pikes Peak and the bowel movement hit him about this part of Alabama and they named it Dugton" (29). She worries that Jed will "be stuck for life" in what she calls "this here dum hellhole" (29). But Jed's mother is talking about geographical escape. Jed wants more. He cannot see that place is inescapable; it is familial, spiritual, and self-defining. Jed wishes to deny that he was born in Dugton, that his father was a womanizer and drunkard, but more important, that he bears the imprimatur of human limitation by an existence that began in Dugton.

Jed's childhood escape is Latin. His teacher's explanation for why she loved the language is that "it sort of took you out of yourself" (32). Jed's love for the language had a more specific purpose. "In Claxford County, reality," he says, "had been bleached away. But if you found a new name for a thing, it became real. That was the magic of the name"(31). Jed seeks new names for reality in order to change reality. But Latin fails him. Jed paints a pathetic picture of himself and Miss McClatty working their language together: "We lean over the book together, two deprived ones, two crippled ones, two wanderers in a world of shadows, each trying to set eye to a mystic peephole that may give on a bright reality beyond" (33). They are deprived of any sense of place in the present and any sense of self-awareness. Latin, for Jed, is an abstraction of reality and allows one seemingly to stand outside time, escape all responsibility for who and what he is. Jed creates an illusory life for himself that relieves him from all responsibility to reality.

Jed escapes the rural South that he has grown to despise and continues his formal education at the University of Chicago. Physically, he has new surroundings, but his new place is an "unspecifiable destination" (49). Jed is beginning to feel a certain placelessness. He laments his new location, "I was free in my loneliness, for I was lonely for nothing" (59). He is situated but is not grounded; without place, life is meaningless.

Jed is to study Romance Languages at the University of Chicago. He discovers that through languages he can create fictive yet powerful "places to come to" that allow for escapes from Dugton. A graduate professor, Heinrich Stahlmann, introduces Jed to the "*imperium intellectus*," which is the highest form of mental abstraction. The professor describes it, "As the *Civitas Dei*, for the Christian, sheds light on the cities of men, so the *imperium intellectus* may illuminate and quicken the world of our bewildered body and bestial members"(73). Jed is thrilled at his new discovery. He confides to Stahlmann about his origins, "We were poor. Dirt-poor. My father was a handsome, illiterate fool in overalls who wanted something that was not for him in Claxford County, Alabama, or in the whole goddamned world, and he was a drunkard, and died drunk" (69-79). Jed admits his place of origin to Stahlmann because he believes that he has escaped it. He is no longer from Dugton. The *imperium intellectus* provides Jed with a new sense of place. Ironically, he defines his "new" place by reference to Dugton. Jed has discovered another illusory world much like the "world of shadows" provided by Latin.

Jed leaves the University to fight in the war. His commission takes him to Italy. While there, Jed murders a German officer who demonstrates an awareness of self-identity and a commitment to place that Jed sorely lacks. When asked to tell the location of friends or die, the officer exclaims, "Heil Hi--" and Jed kills him. Why? "Not so much because he hated him," says Jed, but because "I envied him" (86). Jed kills the German officer because he has the homeland, the *patria*, that Jed refuses to acknowledge. In Italy, Jed is farther away from Alabama, geographically, than he has ever been, but Jed cannot escape his identity. Each event of his life interpreted Jed in relation to place. He is called home to Dugton again and again, if only in memory. Part of the chapter is narrated in the third person. The fragmented nature of the main action demonstrates the lack of wholeness in Jed's life (82). Also, the third person narration suggests his embarrassment with his life and an actual attempt by the author, Jed, to escape the telling of his personal life.[17]

Jed comes to Nashville after the war and assumes a teaching position at Vanderbilt. Rozelle Hardcastle is in Nashville. She had been the belle of Dugton and had made it her goal to escape the southern town's poverty and backward ways. She is married to Lawford Carrington, the wealthiest man in Nashville. Rozelle and Jed have an affair. They find in each other a common identity because they share a place of origin. "It was the reality of the jealous pain at her past that, somehow, was the sanctuary I could flee to, to escape the unreality of my own" (236). Jed calls their affair, "devised plummetings into timeless sexuality" (313). Their moments together are, "outside the texture of actuality, outside of Time, we seemed, . . . paradoxically, to be living in the meaningfulness of time" (261).

Jed has discovered another illusory world and this time has an accomplice. Yet they have not discovered the "meaningfulness of time;" rather, they have discovered an escape from Dugton, an illusory substitute for grief and loss of identity. Their coupling is passionless and mechanical. Rozelle lies listlessly during the act, one arm over her eyes. Jed is the active partner, the character passionate for an identity which he longs to find in a relationship with someone from Dugton. In his relationship with Rozelle, Jed seeks a substitute for Dugton. But Rozelle, in a moment of disgust over her origins, ironically exclaims the truth about her and Jed. "No matter how rich I am, I know I'm just Dugton" (305).

Jed leaves Nashville seeking an "escape into time, into its routines and nags, which make life possible after all" (313). His escape into time will eventually lead him to an affirmation of his past and, in turn, to an awareness of an identity that will allow Jed to meet the moral challenge of the tragic existence. His escape into time must lead him to his past. Diane Bonds explains, "Jed must recover his past

before he can imbue his experiences with meaning and value. Only by
confronting his past does Jed achieve a wholeness of vision through
which he can approach wholeness of being."[18]

His life becomes anxious and restless. Jed suffers from an absence
in his life of any "place to come to" that gives meaning to his
existence. Throughout the novel, he seems "trapped" in "some
irreversible process" as if he were "coffee beans dropped in a coffee
grinder as big as the world" (20). Jed wishes to escape more than the
human limitation of place; Jed wishes to escape time. He fears more
than being "tied to" Dugton. He fears being connected to the human
family. He escapes Dugton to escape mortality, and he runs from his
father who serves as a metaphor for Jed's finitude.

Jed cannot accept the embarrassment and the fear that comes with
his father's death. The death of his father is a reflection of his own
finitude, the human limitation of time. His father "got killed in the
middle of the night standing up in the front of his wagon to piss on the
hindquarters of one of a span of mules and, being drunk, pitching
forward on his head, still hanging on to his dong, and hitting the pike
in such a position and condition that both the left front and the left rear
wheels of the wagon rolled, with perfect precision, over his
unconscious neck, his having passed out being, no doubt, the reason he
took the fatal plunge in the first place. Throughout, he was still
holding on to his dong" (9).

His father's death becomes the subject of ridicule. The sheer
embarrassment at the way his father died is one source of Jed's desire to
leave home. The accident happens when he is nine. Jed discovers his
hate for his father in the school yard (28), where peers taunt and jeer at
him and make fun of his father's death. So even as a child, Jed wishes
to step outside of time and escape certain embarrassing events that come
with being from Dugton. His father's death becomes the excuse he
needs to leave home.

More important, Jed wishes to step outside of time and escape his
own finitude. To accept his father's death is to accept his own
inevitable death. Jed flees family, his father, in order to flee his own
mortality. He will spend a lifetime reclaiming a lineage, a place in the
human family as "Old Buck's" son, and claiming the human limitation
of finitude that is part of being in the human family. With birth comes
an unavoidable embeddedness in a heritage and in a relationship to the
human community. The death of his father makes this relationship all
the more real to Jed.

On the day of his father's funeral, Jed recalls a scene some years earlier, riding on a wagon with his father, "I remember distinctly the retarded, inexorable grind of the gravel under the iron tires, a sound that seemed to declare some irreversible process in which we were trapped." This "irreversible process" is human mortality. He remembers his father's pained cry as they rode along, "Jesus--what a man is" (19-20)! "What a man is," is a creature limited by the nature of his finitude and who must do the best in life with what little of worth life offers. Jed tries to make sense of his life. He says, "we are all stuck with trying to find the meaning of our lives, and the only thing we have to work on, or with, is our past. This can be a question of life and death" (24). Jed's past represents the death of his father and Jed's own tie to human finitude.

Jed tries to escape the "likes of men," the world of his father. Yet one cannot escape time and its indiscriminating effects on the human creature. While at the University of Chicago, Jed performs "a character sketch of his father, ending the performance on his feet to enact, in much the same spirit as his old torture of the school yard, the hilarious episode of his father's death, complete with hand on hypothetical dong and the lethal plunge" (26). And, as he points out, "he was a social success" (26). Jed's mock killing of his father and his acceptance into the Chicago social circle do very little to bring him peace. The irony is that Jed's success is brought about by an awareness of his past, particularly his father's death. Jed's university experience brings him his first real awareness of human finitude. His major professor, Stahlmann, commits suicide because of what he saw as a failure to return to Germany and "claim my patrimony of honor" (75). Stahlmann, a German Jew, is aware that a person's identity is bound to a *father*--land. He does not have the courage to face his denial of identity and kills himself.

Jed marries while attending the university. His wife, Agnes, contracts cancer. His escape from her pain is to delve deeper into his work and her death gives his work meaning. He writes an essay on "Dante and the Metaphysics of Death." Jed's understanding of death comes out of his daily observations of Agnes' process of dying and his own understanding of Dante's poetry. He publishes the text and soon becomes a well respected scholar. Nevertheless, he finds no answers to self-identity in his fame, nor does he learn from Agnes' death. While he feeds off of her illness, Jed is not aware that he too suffers from the human situation of finitude. He mistakenly thinks that her death has given him self-identity, but it has only given him reputation. Not

until he confronts and accepts his father's death does Jed begin to
establish his identity. As he buries Agnes in South Dakota, he
realizes, "Ripley City, its ways were not the ways of Dugton,
Alabama" (116).

Jed will find peace with himself and a sense of self-identity only
by resurrecting his father and accepting his father's place as an extension
of Jed's own place within a time-bound human family. Jed must
become aware, painfully so, that the limitations of his father are, in a
fundamental way, his limitations too.

IV

In *A Place to Come To* self-identity is inextricably bound to the
human limitations of place and finitude, space and time. Jed's life is
tragic because of his limitations. Yet his life "takes on" a tragic
nobility when he accepts his limitations and endures their imposition
on his existence. The tragic dimension adds richness to existence.
Richard Howard explains that "on the one hand, we exist only by
getting on with it, only by continuity; yet on the other hand, only by
discontinuity do we know we exist."[19] Tragedy brings about a
qualitative difference that is important in one's life. Jed cannot
overcome his limitations; he must live "in spite of" them. Unable to
reject or ignore them, he must be accountable to them. Jed learns that
human limitation is the most critical characteristic of self-definition.
He comes to accept place of origin and his own finitude. Through
courage he attains a level of nobility.

Jed gains a more profound understanding of his life when his
relationship with his own son brings about a more profound
understanding of and appreciation for his dead father. The limitations
imposed upon him by place and finitude, limitations for which his
father serves as symbol, Jed now passes on to his own son. He
discovers that these limitations are the distinguishing characteristics of
being human, and that while they serve to limit a person, they also
serve to define a person's existence. Jed returns home, to Dugton,
Alabama, and accepts his place of origin and his relationship to his
father and, in turn, discovers self-identity. He now enters the world,
accepting his human limitations, facing those limitations with courage,
and willing to live his life "in spite" of human fate.

Jed, having exhausted himself in search of the one incident in his
life that will give self-knowledge, finds himself back in Chicago.
Noteworthy is that Jed returns to the place that took him away from
Dugton to confess his need for his hometown. He contacts an old

Chicago friend, a physicist, Stephen Mostoski, who is away from his own homeland, Poland. Jed tells Stephen of his dislike for Dugton, of his ever present pain for not returning. He tells him also of his embarrassment at not taking Ephriam, a son from a failed marriage, to see his grandmother. Jed obviously fears Dugton, what the town may say about who he is, a Southerner born in poverty, marked by accent, and bound to a geographical region that suggests ignorance and squalor. He fears his dead father, whose death has become symbolic of Jed's own mortality.

Stephen confronts Jed with a truth about Ephriam and him. "You did him a grave injustice . . . I can imagine his wanting to go with you--to see you--his father . . . be reborn" (373). The idea of rebirth is significant. Rebirth involves an acceptance of origins, identity, and one's place in the human community. Mostoski makes Jed realize that the material and spiritual worlds are inseparable. Jed knows this and had known it since the birth of his own son. Ephriam's birth caused Jed to recall his own father. "Had there been a time, before the panther-piss took hold, when Old Buck Tewksbury--when young Buck Tewksbury, . . . crept at night into a darkened room and stood to look down at a black-haired male infant in an improvised cradle, sucking, no doubt, at its thumb or a sugar-tit" (335)? Jed is awaking to the involuntary connection that all persons have to the human community. He, too, has marked his child with inescapable origins and family in the same manner that Old Buck marked him. Jed begins the process of affirming his past, of claiming what Neil Nakadate calls its "enduring value . . . the continuity of human identities in the present and for the future."[20]

With the moment of Jed's courageous decision to accept his tie to Alabama comes the novel's epiphany scene. Jed is in Chicago. During a late evening stroll, Jed sees a young man attack an elderly Italian woman. Jed rushes to her assistance. He is stabbed by the thief and before he loses consciousness he sees the young man leap to the hood of a car, "his pale yellow face lifted to the high stars, his lips open in a wildly beautiful, lyric, birdlike cry of triumph, an angelic, gratuitous and beastful cry to the stars. I remember thinking how beautiful, how redemptive, it all seemed. It was as though I loved him . . . he moved like Ephriam . . . I thought how all the world was justified in that moment" (381). Jed recognizes the common tie of all persons to the human family. Each of us is "everyman." Jed spends the evening in the hospital with the old woman. She calls him son; he does not protest. She is the mother Jed refused to return to; now he is the faithful child. Having earned a sense of respectability as a son, he now has the courage to return to Alabama and make peace with his family, his roots, and his identity.

In a moving scene, he stands before the graves of his mother and father with "the wild impulse to lie on the earth between the two graves, the old and the new, and stretch out a hand to each" (393). He doesn't simply choose Dugton; he embraces it. Jed enters time,--the past, present, and future--and takes responsibility for his place in it. He has sought and found his identity, and a moral order is reflected in his newly found commitment to self and to the human endeavor of love and community that transcends the self. Jed has the courage to take charge of his life in spite of life's tragic dimensions.

Jed's new sense of self sheds light on "a fundamental aspect of man's nature" and the human experience, that "men are real, and brothers in their reality" (393), and that a person must have the courage to return to a "final self" (385) and accept responsibility for his origin and tie to the human community. Jed explains his discovery, "a father may not be entirely without worth" (395). Now a father himself, such a statement is an affirmation of his own self-worth.

Jed's return to Alabama is emotional and anxious; he has not been there since he left as a teenager. Jed enters time and place of origin and discovers self. "The only thing I could think of confessing was that I was I" (391). He promises to arrange the funeral for his step-father, Perk Simms, a vicarious act for the true father he failed to recognize. Jed discovers that his mother had made peace with her origins and had asked to be buried next to Jed's father. Her confession is Jed's confession. She explains to Perk, her second, husband who is hurt by his wife's wish to be buried next to her former husband:

> She said, please, to understand, that if something in yore past time was good even a little time, it deserves you not to spit on it, no matter how bad it turned out, she did not want to see anything good ever happened to her throwed away like dirt . . . Both the happiness and the miserableness I learned when I was young, it was that that make me ready to set my heart on you when you come by, Pore Ole Clabber-Head (389).

One cannot deny the past and must take responsibility for it. Such acts take courage and stand as affirmations of life and human dignity. Says Jed's mother, "Dying--shucks!" If you kin handle the living, what's to be afraid of the dying" (390).

Jed accepts the living, but his acceptance comes slowly. He stands before the graves of his father and mother and asks if it is too late to reclaim his past and his family.

> Was it all too late? Was all too late, after all? I had the wild impulse to lie on the earth between the two graves, the old and the new, and stretch out a hand to each. I thought that if I could do that, I might be able to weep, and if I could weep, something warm and blessed might happen. But I did not lie down. The trouble was, I was afraid that nothing might happen, and I was afraid to take the risk. (393)

Jed returns to the place of shame, the place of the "lethal header with the noble dong in clutch." He affirms the very act that caused him to reject his father. Recalling the incident, Jed utters, "Poor Buck", a sad yet humane recognition that he is Buck's son. Now Jed possesses the courage to enter into the human community. Back in Chicago he writes his ex-wife a letter saying: "I ask for your company because it is what I feel myself most deeply craving" (395).

Walker points out that Warren's "books are about human happiness and how it may be achieved by discovering love through knowledge."[21] It takes courage to gain and to accept knowledge about oneself. Jed accepts being Old Buck's son. Now, with remarkable courage he seeks to plunge on in a world tragic and happenstance. Richard Grey points out that Jed's is a "recognition of responsibility, an acceptance of human fallibility, and above all a realization that the personality is complex and finds-indeed creates--itself through a continuous relationship with others."[22] Jed comes to his existential crisis. He can choose life responsibly with all its ups and downs or resign himself to the unfeeling flow of time that makes pawns of human beings. Jed, by seeking companionship, chooses life and affirms the noble dignity of the human creature and his ability to endure the tragic dimensions of life.

V

Robert Penn Warren's tragic-religious world view is well grounded in twentieth century, liberal, Protestant theology. Paul Tillich represents an established theological position that is similar to Warren's religious views.[23] Tillich finds dignity and meaning in the human creature's courageous affirmation of existence and in the decision to face life head on and responsibly, "in spite of" the ever present fears of guilt, meaninglessness, and finitude that pervade human existence.

Tillich and Warren agree that human existence has a tragic dimension and, furthermore, that the tragic dimension of life is uniquely bound to a religious element of existence.[24] Tillich says that the human loss of innocence, the move from "essence to existence" or, in more traditional language "the Fall," involves ethical character that is "derived from daily experiences of people under special cultural and social conditions."[25] The "transition" from essence to existence involves an act of free moral decision on the part of the individual, yet the decision has "a claim to universal validity."[26] While the estrangement from essence is an individual act by an "isolated individual . . . it is an act of freedom which is embedded . . . in the universal destiny of existence."[27] Because estrangement is by personal choice, the human creature must, ultimately, accept responsibility for his/her loss of essence. A person is limited by nature of existence but is nonetheless responsible for those limitations and how he/she deals with those limitations.

Jed is responsible for his estrangement. He chooses to reject his father and to deny any tie to a universal destiny. He is inextricably bound to the human community, its dignity as well as its tragic elements. Jed's tragic flaw is a failure to acknowledge his relationship to the human family. Not only does he reject his father and family, but also flees his homeland, geographically as well as intellectually and spiritually; he denies a place of birth. He now must have courage to reclaim his familial and spiritual inheritance, his "place" with family that tells him who he is.

Courage, for Tillich, "is self-affirmation 'in-spite-of,' that is, in spite of that which tends to prevent the self from affirming itself."[28] Such courage involves the wisdom to know oneself, a willingness to affirm one's origin and nature. Jed is faced with the moral decision of whether to choose resignation and lose himself to the flux of time and, therefore, have existence defined by limiting externals or to choose action and affirm life in spite of its limitations. By choosing life, he uses the few tools at hand, place, family, and relationships, to construct and identity that results in an affirmation of self. To use Warren's metaphor of the card game, one either deals or is dealt to (176-7).

Tillich would suggest that anxiety caused by the human predicament of finitude, meaninglessness, and guilt lures Jed, throughout the novel, towards "non-being," a loss of self and identity. Human fragility is a constant threat to undermine all acts of courage. Jed faces frustrations time and time again when seeking self-knowledge.

"Existentially everybody is aware of the complete loss of self which biological extinction implies."[29] Jed molds his life in response to and in fear of his own and other's finitude. Finitude is life's tragic dimension, and all of life is contingent upon it. He rejects his father because his father dies and leaves. More important, his father's death tells Jed that he too is mortal. Jed leaves his mother and the South because of his father's death. He builds his academic reputation by writing a thesis substantively informed by watching his wife die. Not until Jed is close to death, himself, stabbed while assisting the old woman, does he sense the informative nature of one's mortality. He chooses to live and to exert "the courage to affirm himself in spite of it [finitude]."[30] Jed has a new vision of the world and can return to Dugton to seek forgiveness and reaffirmation of self.

A sense of meaninglessness and emptiness haunts Jed's life. Jed loses his spiritual center when he leaves Dugton and rejects his "place" of origin. "The anxiety of meaninglessness," says Tillich, "is anxiety about the loss of an ultimate concern, of a meaning which gives meaning to all meanings."[31] For Warren the meaning that gives meaning to existence is one's inevitable tie to the human family. Jed must return to Dugton and responsibly affirm his place alongside his father and mother.

The human family with all its frailty and limitations is, for Warren, what Tillich calls "a spiritual center."[32] Jed surrenders himself to this "spiritual center," the human family, and in turn begins to shape his reality, "both his world and himself, according to meanings and values"[33] that are part of what it means to be human. Jed demonstrates various talents for avoiding meaning. He loses himself in his work, seeks abstraction in sex and drink, and escapes to foreign countries. Yet all attempts to avoid reality bring greater anxiety. A person must have a "spiritual center."

Guilt is a result of a person's inability to achieve his/her potential. Jed forges "meanings and values" for himself and his world, yet he must be responsible for his future. The point of one's life, says Tillich, is "what he has made of himself."[34] Jed's ceaseless wanderings do no more than force constant recall of his childhood. He laments his father's death and remembers his mother's love and how long it has been since he has seen her. According to Tillich, a person is "to make of himself what he is supposed to become, to fulfill his destiny."[35] If one does not, an awareness of "ambiguity" develops in his/her life. Jed can "fulfill his destiny" only by returning to Dugton, recognizing spatial limitation and his need for "a place to come to." By not returning, he creates the anxiety of guilt. He is aware of the right thing to do, yet he fails to do it. Until he musters the courage to confront his guilt and chooses to return to his "spiritual center," Jed will live with ambiguity.

Jed lives most of his life estranged from a spiritual center or "ground of being." Warren's development of character is in the form of the quest, a quest for the essential element of life that gives existence meaning. Jed needs courage, the "courage to be," to affirm his identity with the human family, the courage to assert that all "men were real, and brothers in their reality." This reality is an awareness of human limitations. Tillich calls these limitations finitude, guilt, and meaninglessness, while Warren suggest they are space and time. Each believes that these limiting characteristics are endemic to the human situation. The place to come to, in Warren's novel, is a spiritual center, a familial tie to all humanity that grants one the courage to live responsibly and productively in spite of seemingly overwhelming odds and in spite of life's tragic sense. Only with courage can Jed make his home in the "land of the brave."

CHAPTER 5

LITERATURE, LIFE, AND A CRITICAL APPROACH: A PROLEGOMENON

Alasdair MacIntyre points out that "man is in his actions and practices, as well as his fictions, essentially a story-telling animal."[1] People fashion worlds through story, worlds in which men and women seek the good life. Their quests are their narrative histories which involve the discovery of a virtue or virtues to live by that give them the good life they seek. We tell stories not so much to entertain--though stories certainly do entertain---but rather to reveal something about ourselves and to discover what gives identity, purpose, and meaning to our existence.

Implicit in my argument throughout the text is that narrative has life-like characteristics. Narrative is not the sole possession of the novelist but is central to who and what we are as human creatures and is critical to how we understand the world. Narrative, by extension is simply best put to use and finds its most artistically profound expression in the novel.

For this reason, I make the claim that narrative fiction and lived narrative are intricately connected and that lived fiction is the thing of which narrative fiction is made. Both have an intricate structure composed of similar narrative elements. Both lived narrative and fiction are motivated by desire. Each has at its center the element of character(s) who, motivated by desire for wholeness and unity of life, seeks a virtue which makes life livable and complete. Lived narrative, like fiction, reveals a particular virtue by which life is ordered and finds meaning.

I am responding to a current theory of art, of which Ortega y Gasset was aware three decades ago, whose intention is: "1. to dehumanize art; 2. to avoid living forms; 3. to see to it that the work of art is nothing but a work of art; 4. to consider art as play and nothing else; 5. to be essentially ironical; 6. to beware of sham and hence to aspire to scrupulous realization; 7. to regard art as a thing of no transcending consequence."[2] I do not totally accept these pronouncements that are vital to much of modern literary scholarship. Several are critical and important to the post-modern literary task. For example, meaning, religious or otherwise, should not be simple and obvious. Wayne Booth comments about Henry James that "for him mere 'rendering' of surfaces is not enough," nor is "the mere illusion of reality in itself," enough.[3] Meaning in the text is there because "the author's voice is never really silenced."[4] The voice may not, probably is not, the voice the author intends. It may be the voice of history or environment, but the voice is there and means something. Narrative structure allows the voice, meaning, to be heard while text and reader discover purpose and intention together.

My conclusion unfolds in two stages. First I examine the relationship of lived narrative to narrative fiction. In particular, I explore three ways to discuss literature's relations to lived narrative: literature as an extension of lived narrative, Barbara Hardy; life as narrative history, Alasdair MacIntyre; lived narrative and narrative fiction as revealers and portrayers of virtue, Stanley Hauerwas. Second, I address the question, "Can literature mean anything at all?" The question is essential because the validity of the three preceding chapters of this work depends on the answer, yes! Literature must mean in order to express religious value. Therefore, the chapter concludes with a defense of value-oriented literary criticism and suggests a prolegomenon to a hermeneutical method that allows the literary critic to address the "meaning of a text" from a post-modern, critical perspective.

I

Barbara Hardy

Barbara Hardy's argument is straightforward, "Narrative, like lyric or dance, is not to be regarded as an aesthetic invention used by artists to control, manipulate, and order experience, but as a primary act of mind transferred to art from life. The novel merely heightens, isolates, and analyzes the narrative motions of human consciousness."[5] The novel serves as a testing ground for human experience. Like Frank Kermode, Hardy believes that the novel can serve to create order, perhaps an order we cannot trust; nonetheless, it is an order that suggests a sense of wholeness and completion where life in its unpredictability refuses to do so. Narrative plays a psychological function by revealing meaning where there seemingly is none. She writes, "In order really to live, we make up stories about ourselves and others."[6] These stories may find their way to fiction, but they have their origins in life. According to Hardy, we are narratives, for we dream in narrative, daydream in narrative, remember, anticipate, hope, despair, believe, doubt, plan, revise, criticize, construct, gossip, learn, hate, and love by narrative.[7]

Literature is an act of discovery because life is. Fiction becomes a way, by extension, of sorting-out life's queries, chaos, and uncertainty and of finding a way to live with vicissitude. Hardy explains, "We tell stories in order to change, remaking the past in a constant and not always barren *esprit d'escalier*."[8] By no means am I suggesting that the author's task is a simple one. Technique seeks order and does not impose it. The discovery of an ordered existence is not assured. Fiction is subtle and confusing. Like life, there are plots and subplots, narratives within narratives. Hardy describes a work of Henry James in which "the narrative contains a narrative of what happens counterpointed on a narrative of what seems to be happening, or what the spectator tells himself is happening."[9]

The novel has narrative elements because life does. The element of character is critical; it is responsible for narrative action. A character anticipates, dreams, invents, recognizes, discovers. Yet plotting is critical also. The imposition of order is an act of plot and involves some sense of *telos* or conclusion to existence or at least the episodes of existence. A plot's movement need not be chronological. In fact, if fiction is about narrative consciousness, it probably confuses ideas of chronological time. Narrative may be informed by a *telos*, but it first must discover what the telos is. Time, in this sense rambles, frustratingly, around beginnings, middles, and ends, not progressively through them.

Narrative fictions are limited in the same manner that our lives are limited, as Hardy points out, "by our sensibility, inhibitions, language, history, intelligence."[10] Persons in life and literature are shaped by response to their limitations. Stories serve to define existence. The novel, as extension of lived narrative, addresses the critical questions of the life story, "How do I find meaning in life?" Fiction reveals a character in search of self, in discovery of meaning, and in the process of creating order out of disorder. The novel's success and value to the reader depends on the keen mind that works through the confusion of the text and that deciphers some relevance in the story because the story of the text is experientially his/her story.

I find Hardy's argument forceful though she fails to give enough credit to the artist who is responsible for the novel's structure. Hardy implies that an author is overcome by life's narrative nature when putting the text together. I do agree that narrative fiction's relationship to lived narrative should not be a pivotal argument for "author intention" as the most responsible type of literary criticism. But I do think that the artist has more control over his/her craft than Hardy suggests. Indeed, an artist writes from an historical context, and as Crites points out, "the forms of cultural expressions are not historical accidents."[11] Yet Hardy's analysis of narrative's relation to life and fiction is helpful.

Alasdair MacIntyre

To understand the whole, the unity of human life, existence must be placed in a narrative context. Life is narrative, and to tell someone something about life is to tell a story. In *After Virtue*, Alasdair MacIntyre writes that "any answer to the question of how we are to understand or to explain a given segment of behavior will presuppose some prior answer to the question of how these different correct answers to the question, 'What is he doing?' are related to each other."[12] The human creature can never be separated from who he/she was, is, and will be. Any definition of self, says MacIntyre, must be "a concept of a self whose unity resides in the unity of a narrative which links birth to life to death as narrative beginning to middle to end."[13] Thus, life's narrative has as its critical element a character who, in confrontation with life's troubled moments, must make decisions that reveal virtues by which to live his/her life. Life requires decision-making. The decision-making is situational and is a process of discovery in which the good life is revealed. A virtue is "believed in" as a defining condition of one's existence.

Life is situated within a structure of its own narrative elements, setting, atmosphere, tone, and character. The setting is perhaps one's profession, one's place of birth, one's familial surroundings. According to MacIntyre settings make the actions of characters "intelligible both to agents themselves and to others."[14] Where we live, whom we know, and the things we do are contextual and give sensibility to our actions. Yet as in literature, setting is merely a part of a greater narrative. "Setting has a history," says MacIntyre.[15] Families, traditions, and professions that are most notably part of a person's current existence are, in reality, a part of a person's total story. Thus a chronology of past, present, and future embodies each character's life narrative.

Human beings are situated in settings in which time, says MacIntyre, "is ordered both casually and temporally."[16] The ordering of time gives life its sense of plot, and allows a person to understand his/her narrative history, past, present, and future. "What I am," says MacIntyre, "therefore, is in key part what I inherit, a specific past that is present to some degree in my present."[17] He suggests that this plotting effect helps a person write a history, "In determining what causal efficacy the agent's intentions had in one or more directions, and how his short-term intentions succeeded or failed to be constitutive of long-term intentions, we ourselves write a further part of these histories."[18]

Each human being is limited by social and personal circumstances in the quest for the virtuous life. In narrative fiction these limitations I have called atmosphere. MacIntyre points out that we each bear a "particular social identity."[19] Each belongs to a particular country, a particular family. Each of us, I add, is finite. The list is endless. Life has "its own moral particulars." We discover who and what we are because of limitations.

Our lives have a 'tone' to them because of situation, chronology, and limitations. If tone is the orientation of the teller towards the tale, how we respond to life, as a character, sets the tone of our existence. We have no choices but to respond to existence, our places in time. "What I have called a history," says MacIntyre, "is an enacted dramatic narrative in which the characters are also the authors."[20] The individual is the point of view of his/her life. A person's response to life, whether noble, tragic, bitter, gives to life its tone.

Life's narrative structure reveals the human desire for a *telos*. The desire for completion, a sense of emotional and intellectual wholeness to life, is what gives lived narrative its religious sense. MacIntyre explains that our lives have "a certain teleological character."[21] Each person has an awareness of a future or, in relation to others, "a possible shared future."[22] This future takes on religious and moral implications when it informs and guides existence. "There is no present," says MacIntyre, "which is not informed by some image of some future and an image of the future which always presents itself in the form of a *telos*--or a variety of ends or goals--towards which we are either moving or failing to move in the present."[23] Life needs a sense of *denouement*. This awareness of a *telos* is the way in which future informs the present.

Discovery is an essential element of life's narrative structure. Coexistent with teleology, says MacIntyre, is life's unpredictability. "We do not know what will happen next, but nonetheless our lives have a certain form which projects itself towards our future."[24] I suggest that this "form which projects itself" is life's narrative structure in the process of discovery of that virtue that best informs existence. Lived narrative is the process of asking, "What is the good life?" The question presents a person with myriad possibilities for answers as well as the possibility for discovery. While a *telos* may give one some indication of what a good person or a good life is, even a *telos* is established only in the process of questioning and deciding. MacIntyre points out that "it is in looking for a conception of *the* good, which will enable us to order other goods."[25] Lived narrative is a process of questioning and discovery. Life is a narrative quest and is motivated by a desire for the good. Lived narrative unfolds within a context of existential crises. In response, persons seek the good life and discover a virtue with which to overcome or endure the situation. This event establishes the virtue by which, if only for the moment, a person lives his/her life and establishes a world-view that informs existence through or until the next crisis. MacIntyre notes that we discover a "conception of the good that will enable us to understand the place of integrity and constancy in life," so that we can "define the kind of life which is a quest for the good."[26] This is the function of lived narrative and the function of narrative fiction.

The belief that the newly discovered virtue can and will order one's life for a qualitatively better existence gives MacIntyre's lived narrative its religious dimension. One acts on beliefs. One accepts and lives-out newly discovered virtues, says MacIntyre, which "will not only sustain practices and enable us to achieve the goods intended to practices, but which will also sustain us in the relevant kind of quest for the good, by enabling us to overcome harms, dangers, temptations, and distractions which we encounter, and which will furnish us with increasing self-knowledge and increasing knowledge of the good."[27] The act of belief is implicitly a religious act. Lived narrative, like narrative fiction, is a quest for something to believe in, for an answer to the question, "What is the good life?" The structure of lived narrative, suggests MacIntyre, leads to a discovery of an answer to this question.

Stanley Hauerwas

Stanley Hauerwas suggests that to live the virtuous life is to live faithful to a story--particularly, for Hauerwas, the Christian story.[28] The virtuous person must be situated in a narrative, embedded in a story. Hauerwas explains: "when 'acts' are abstracted from history, the moral self cannot help but appear as an unconnected series of actions lacking continuity and unity."[29] With MacIntyre, Hauerwas believes that narrative brings structure and unity to existence. The story takes on all the dramatic elements of narrative, and a character is the critical element for moral and religious development. "The self is the subject of growth," says Hauerwas. Narrative "renders a character"[30] and demonstrates the virtue required for "moral development."[31]

Critical for Hauerwas' understanding of narrative and the virtuous life is the idea that a character and a narrative are essential to moral growth. By character he means "self determining beings, who act upon and through their nature and environment to give their lives particular form."[32] The definition is important for Hauerwas because the definition implies that a person "is more than that which simply happens to him, for he has the capacity to determine himself beyond momentary excitation and acts."[33] A character makes decisions that are accountable to the story of the community of which he/she is a part. Decision making is crucial. According to Hauerwas, "the descriptions of 'situations' do not come as givens, but are parts of a larger narrative whole."[34] "Situations" require decisive response that informs the narrative whole. Hauerwas claims that "no matter what narrative we do find ourselves in or what virtues we have acquired, we do find ourselves having to make choices that require justification."[35] He does not suggest that community imposes virtue on a character, an action that defeats the purpose of narrative altogether. Rather the story of the community is the narrative through which a person discovers the virtuous and good life. Hauerwas points out that in the Christian community there must be imposed on a character "neither a singly moral principle nor a harmony of the virtues; " rather, what takes place is "the formation of character by a narrative that provides a sufficiently truthful account of our existence."[36]

Narrative serves to situate the human being in a history--alive and ongoing--that defines his/her character and allows for that character in response to his/her narrative history to discover the good life. Hauerwas writes, "The self is best understood as a narrative, and normatively we require a narrative that will provide the skills appropriate to the conflicting loyalties and roles we necessarily confront in our existence."[37] Narrative reveals to us boundaries, plots, and settings by which we interpret our character and the virtuous life.

"The unity of the self," says Hauerwas, "is therefore more like the unity that is exhibited in a good novel."[38] We define ourselves by telling our personal stories in response to a larger story about human existence, by "having," says Hauerwas, "a narrative that gives us skills of interpretation sufficient to allow us to make our past our own through incorporation into our ongoing history."[39] Whether lived

narrative or narrative fiction, our stories require a narrative structure, a
way "to make sense" of our lives. And like narrative fiction, a character
makes decisions within a history that reveals self-identity, a place in a
particular history, and a dominant virtue within that history that can
inform existence. Decisions are made that reveal "who I am" and "what
I can be," and most important, the good life. Virtuous existence is the
telos of the self-identity question, and as Hauerwas points out, the *telos*
itself is a narrative.[40]

Hauerwas believes that narrative fiction is an excellent paradigm
for self-discovery and exploring the virtuous life. Because self-unity is
like "a good novel," the close examination of good fiction, with a focus
on a character's development, can shock us into recognition of
ourselves. Observing characters in novels, we can encounter and learn
from lived narrative's reflection in narrative fiction. The significance of
the novel for lived narrative is its reflective power. Because we are
narrative beings, situated in a history, we are best able to respond
morally to another narrative. Because the novel is narrative, it is, says
Hauerwas, "epistemologically crucial."[41]

A novel need not depend totally on realism for its success. Yet
the novel must be realistic enough to entreat sympathy. "No novel is
anything . . . unless the reader can sympathize with characters whose
names he finds upon the page," says Anthony Trollope.[42] More so
than character identity, says Hauerwas, a novel's form demonstrates the
virtue it recommends. A character, as one part of a whole structure,
reveals not simply a person but a way of life that is consistent and
conversational with the way we live our lives. A reader confronts a
narrative world that penetrates his/her own, and because we too are
narrative beings, narrative fiction can equip us with tools of virtue with
which to build our moral and religious lives.

II

Franz Kafka tells us that "if the book we are reading does not
wake us, as with a fist hammering on our skull, why then do we read
it? . . . A book must be an ice-axe to break the sea frozen inside us."
Literature has moral vision and stands in tension with the culture that
produces it and is constructively critical of the norms and values of the
world of which it is a part. Good literature is a way of looking at the
world; it also suggests a way of living in the world. The most critical
question for the literary critic to ask after tireless critical inquiry is,
"What does my work mean?" Annie Dillard says: "It may be naive to
ask what we can learn from *Othello*, but it is decadent not to."[43]

But how do we discuss the moral visions inherent in literature and not stifle the creative imagination nor sound egotistical and dogmatic? The most difficult task, according to David Tracy, is "to encourage creativity in interpretation without forfeiting the need for criteria of adequacy for interpretation."[44] The essential question is, "How do we engage in meaning in a text without losing critical suspicion of that meaning, if not of the text itself?" I am convinced of two things. One, I believe that texts have meaning. Two, we can agree upon methods of critical inquiry that engage this meaning and, at the same time call it into question, strip it of illusion and superficiality, yet never lose sight of some degree of applicability to the human situation.

A text has meaning. Lionel Trilling writes, "The tale is not told by an idiot but by a rational consciousness which perceives in things the processes that are their reason and which derive from this perception a principle of conduct, a way of living among things."[45] We, as critics, need not accept this "principle of conduct" as gospel. Perhaps we merely agree or disagree with a text's meaning. The question of truth need not enter into our engagement with the text. But the world is things and ideas of which texts are made. The writer has at hand bits of the world to manipulate and to arrange in some particular fashion.

Criticism of a text becomes self-defeating if its goal is to suggest that the text has no meaning. The critical task is absurd--perhaps pernicious--if its sole task is to create a meaningful gloss on that which has no meaning to begin with, where, according to Nathan Scott, there is "nothing at all that can be counted on to 'center' language, to limit the 'free-play' of the significatory process, and to establish stable referents outside language for spoken and written utterance."[46] Giles Gunn points out that "if no text contains any core of determinate or restricted meaning but only a field of indeterminate and unrestricted meanings, then the critic's job ceases to be the adjudication of claims between the text's latent and manifest meanings and becomes instead the submission to their endlessly various elaboration . . . The point is to avoid being taken in."[47]

The meaningful exposure of a shallow and incomplete interpretation of a text and the critical tools necessary for such exposure are required of us if we are to be good literary critics. But there is no merit in removing all meaningful foundation from literary texts, in suggesting that language is constructed only of pure differences. Indeed, like Robert Scholes, I am not ready to say that language is not based on differences, but it is also "based upon references."[48] This lost dimension of references is, I suggest, critical to value-oriented literary criticism.

A discussion of meaningful references in literature must consider Wayne Booth's idea of the role of belief in literature. The critic must concur, to some degree, with the beliefs of the text in order to read the text in a credible manner. Booth is explicit, "The implied author of each novel is someone with whose beliefs on all subjects I must largely agree if I am to enjoy his work."[49] While "enjoy" is not the essential task of the literary critic, I do agree that the critic, for a moment, must accept the text's hypothetical world with all its beliefs and assumptions before establishing any critical distance from the text. And certainly with the first reading of a text, that first encounter with a newly fashioned world, isn't it impossible, says Booth, to suggest that "incompatibility of beliefs" with the text is "irrelevant to . . . judgment of the text?"[50] Differences of belief are as critical as concurrence of belief and indeed may lead to a more revealing critical analysis of the text.

Reading a text from the stance of belief implies religious and moral meaning. "To pretend," says Booth, "that we read otherwise, to claim that we can make ourselves into objective, dispassionate, thoroughly tolerant readers is in the final analysis nonsense."[51] Because the text reveals a world of beliefs and assumptions, moral evaluation is invited to be part of textual analysis. A critic cannot avoid value-oriented analysis anymore than a text can avoid portraying a value-oriented world-view. We are subjective creatures. MacIntyre suggests that text and reader enter into a conversation "in which the participants are not only the actors, but also the joint authors, working out in agreement or disagreement the modes of their production."[52] The critic responds to moral claims in the text only because he/she knows, to some extent, what a moral claim is. The critical act is an evaluative act and implies meaning. I agree with Booth that writers see a connection between art and morality, "Their artistic vision consists, in part, of a judgment on what they see, and they would ask us to share that judgment as part of the vision."[53] But if a text suggests "principles of conduct," personal utility, and moral values, yet at the same time interpreters engage the text from a variety of critical stances, how do we preserve the text's integrity?

The answer to the question is found in an interpretation theory that holds in strong tension a "hermeneutics of restoration" with a "hermeneutics of suspicion."[54] I agree that thus far I seem rather obsessed with literature's restorative abilities, that literature tells us something useful about ourselves and shows us holistic ways to live in the world. But I am convinced that in order for the critical act to reclaim meaning and moral vision, it is the hermeneutics of suspicion that is most critical to our endeavor. While texts restore, they also deceive. Scholes explains, "Texts are places where power and weakness become visible and discussable, where learning and ignorance manifest themselves, where the structures that enable and constrain our thoughts and actions become palpable."[55]

The interpretation theory of Hans-Georg Gadamer, interpreted and amended by David Tracy, suggests a pluralistic theory of interpretation that on the one hand says texts are meaningful and on the other hand establishes critical distance from the text in the form of a hermeneutics of suspicion. Tracy's goal for interpretation is a "perspective expressing a dominating interest in universal and elemental features of human existence as those features bear on the human desire for liberation and authentic existence."[56] He desires an approach to the text that is not impositional and is not simply engaged in "avoiding understanding," particularly at the expense of the text's meaning. "Interpretation theory," Tracy explains, must "both encourage creativity and demand criteria for adequacy."

An interpreter comes to the text with prejudgments. One cannot escape historical influences. The most obvious event in history of which we are an inescapable part is language. "No one who thinks in and through a particular language," says Tracy, "escapes the history of the effects--the tradition inevitably present in that language."[57] The text itself makes us aware of these prejudgments we bring to interpretation and how endemic these judgments are. For the text makes a "claim to attention," and causes "vexation" and provocation. Tracy explains that "the actual experience of that claim to attention may range from a tentative sense of resonance with the question posed by the text through senses of import or even shocks of recognition or repugnance elicited by this classic text."[58] His point is that good literature, to a degree, interprets us and, in turn, makes us aware of preconceived ideas and notions.

This claim to attention by the text leads to the step of textual interpretation, Gadamer's model of the "game" of conversation between interpreter and text.[59] We are caught in the "to-and-fro movement of the logic of question and response."[60] For Tracy this is a scheme for "authentic conversation." Interpretation now discovers meaning. Meaning is not found in the text itself, in the prejudgments of the interpreter, nor in the history behind the text. Meaning is found in the conversation between text and interpreter, in the shared questions and answers between interpreter and text. Meaning lives outside the text, more specifically, "in front of the text"--Gadamer's "fused horizon." Obviously, meaning will not be the same for everyone. Interpretation is pluralistic. But what keeps the interpreter from playing a degree of havoc with the text's meaning?

Two correctives are in order. Gadamer shies away from critical method. Not only is it impositional, but it also demands a degree of control over the text which distorts the conversation. Yet precisely because Gadamer believes that both text and interpreter are "steeped in history," critical theory is necessary. The "need for suspicion," "for critical theories," says Tracy, "to spot and heel systematic distortions in our personal--and, beyond that, our cultural and social-lives has become an indispensable aspect of any modern interpreter's horizon of preunderstanding and possibility for creative interpretation."[61] For this reason, structuralists and post-structuralists play an essential role in literary interpretation. These critical theories seek to undo illusion and reveal what Tracy calls the "hidden, repressed, unconscious distortions present in both the preunderstanding of the interpreter and the classic texts and tradition."[62] Yet these theories are essential only to the degree that suspicion leads to restoration, intelligible, profound meaning, and not to some absurd, reductive approach that, rather ironically, systematically calls into question the very possibility that meaning can exist in the text.

The second corrective is most crucial and involves the awareness that texts can tell us how meaning is produced by texts. Criticism takes on creative character. The nature of narrative suggests a critical theory of forms, which is the foundation of my study. Creative critical theory can explain to us how literary expression occurs: genre, style, structure. To resist such theory is "to resist both understanding and creativity." Or, as Tracy explains, "understanding and explanation need not be implacable enemies."[63]

Throughout my study I have argued that the quest for meaning is a religious quest and that the task of the literary critic is to address the question of textual meaning. With the question of meaning comes the question of religion, and we cannot throw out the baby with the bath water. Rather, we affirm that religious questions exist, and we develop the critical tools necessary for their scholarly exploration. With such a view, we take an holistic approach to literary criticism. Critically distant from and humanely close to our work, we practice literary criticism that gives depth to purpose.

NOTES

NOTES TO INTRODUCTION

1. I say "hypothetical" world, as opposed to "fictive" world because hypothetical suggests, more than fictive, that the world revealed by narrative is possible, if not real. A reader, in turn, then tries and tests the hypothesis presented by the narrative. To call the world "fictive" is to suggest that the world described by narrative is not real nor is related to that which is real.

2. I am in agreement with Wesley Kort's suggestion that character, plot, tone, and atmosphere are narrative's major elements and are inclusive of other narrative elements. And I am much indebted to his work on narrative and narrative elements. See Wesley Kort's, *Narrrative Elements and Religious Meaning*. Philadelphia: Fortress, 1975.

3. These world-views are predominantly male, though I give a feminist reading of James Agee's *A Death in the Family* in chapter 2. Yet, at this point, I wish only to describe the religious world-views, not defend them. Further critical work is needed to "deconstruct" what are the dominant and male-oriented religious world-views of the texts.

NOTES TO CHAPTER 1

1. Mircea Eliade, *The Sacred and the Profane*, Trans. Willard R. Trask. (New York: Harper 1961) 210.

2. Eliade, *Sacred* 210.

3. Stephen Crites, "The Narrative Quality of Experience," *Journal of the American Academy of Religion* (1971) 294.

4. Richard Weiman, "'Fictionality' and Realism: Rabelais to Barth," in *The Uses of Fiction*, Douglas Jefferson and Graham Martin, ed. (Milton Keynes: The Open U P, 1982) 19.

5. Frank Kermode, *The Genesis of Secrecy* (Cambridge: Harvard U P, 1979) 122-3.

6. Robert Higbie, *Character and Structure in the English Novel* (Gainesville: U of Florida P, 1984) 8.

7. Wesley Kort, *Narrative Elements and Religious Meaning* (Philadelphia: Fortress, 1975) 6.

8. See Rudolf Otto's, *The Idea of the Holy* (London: Oxford U P, 1923) and Giles Gunn's, *The Interpretation of Otherness* (New York: Oxford U P, 1979).

9. Frank Kermode, *The Sense of an Ending* (London: Oxford U P,1966).

10. Kermode, *Sense* 8.

11. Kermode, *Sense* 35.

12. Kermode, *Sense* iii.

13. I have intentionally personified narrative because I believe that narrative has a "life of its own" and that language can and does seek its own coherence. Of course, language is not "alive," yet it is so integrally a part of what it means to be human that I am comfortable with my personification.

14. Robert Scholes, *Structuralism in Literature* (New Haven: Yale U P, 1974) 112.

15. Mark Schorer, "Technique as Discovery," in *Approaches to the Novel*, Robert Scholes, ed. (San Francisco: Chandler, 1961) 249.

16. Schorer, "Technique" 249.

17. Erich Kahler, *The Inward Turn of Narrative*, Trans. Richard and Clara Winston (Princeton: Princeton U P, 1973) 142f.

18. Ortega y Gasset, *Toward a Philosophy of History* (New York,1941) 214 227-8.

19. See Scholes, *Structuralism*, 154.

20. Stephen Crites, "Angels We Have Heard," in James Wiggins, *Religion as Story* 24.

21. Schorer, "Technique" 255.

22. For an opposing position see Malcolm Bradbury's chapter, "An Approach Through Structure," in *Towards a Poetics of Fiction*, Mark Spilka, ed. (Bloomington: Indiana U P, 1977).

23. Flannery O'Connor, *Mystery and Manners* (New York: Farrar,1969) 100.

24. Schorer, "Technique" 256.

25. Scholes, *Structuralism* 110.

26. Brooks, *Reading* 10.

27. Shlomith, Rimmon-Kenan, *Narrative Fiction: Contemporary Poetics* (New York: Methuen, 1983) 32.

28. Again, I express my debt to the work of Wesley Kort that examines so well the major elements, as well as their functions, of narrative structure.

29. Kort, *Narrative* 1.

30. Kort, *Narrative* 4-6.

31. Kort, *Narrative* 17.

32. See Wesley Kort's text, *Moral Fiber, Character and Belief in Recent American Fiction* (Philadelphia: Fortress, 1982).

33. Paul Ricoeur, *Time and Narrative*, v. 2, Trans. Kathleen McLoughlin and David Pellauer (Chicago: U of Chicago P, 1985) 94.

34. Henry James, *The Art of Fiction and Other Essays*, Morris Roberts, ed. (New York, 1948).

35. Percy Lubbock, *The Craft of Fiction* (New York: Viking, 1960) 251.

36. Gunn, *Interpretation* 84.

37. Kort, *Narrative* 100.

38. Kort, *Narrative* 20.

39. For a more detailed discussion of this observation, see Tzvetan Todorov, *The Poetics of Prose*, Trans. Richard Howard, forward by Jonathan Cueller (New York: Cornell U P, 1977) 226.

40. Eudora Welty, *The Eye of the Story* (New York: Vintage, 1979) 122
41. Kort, *Narrative* 35.
42. Brooks, *Reading* xiii.
43. Brooks, *Reading* xiii.
44. Todorov, *Poetics* 111.
45. Brooks, *Reading* 5.
46. Brooks, *Reading* 7.
47. Brooks, *Reading* 10.
48. Of course closure is not always achieved; nonetheless, closure is almost always desired. Thus even without closure there is tension in the text caused by a wish for closure. For example, see Mark 16.8 in the Christian New Testament.
49. Macauley and Lanning, *Technique* 181.
50. Kermode, *Sense* 45.
51. Kort, *Narrative* 65.
52. Konigsberg, *Technique* 3.
53. Higbie, *Character* 4.
54. Ricoeur, *Time* 36.
55. Higbie, *Character* 16.
56. Ricoeur, *Time* 137.
57. Crites, "Narrative" 303.
58. And again, I wish to emphasize that these religious world-views are traditionally male in orientation and indeed deserve certain critical evaluation from feminist perspectives.
59. See Wilhelm Reich's *The Sexual Revolution* (New York: Farrar, 1945) Trans. Theodore P. Wolfe. See particularly the chapter, "The Compulsive Family as Educational Apparatus."
60. Walter Rauschenbusch, *A Theology for the Social Gospel* (Nashville: Abingdon, 1978) 54.
61. Rauschenbusch, *A Theology* 155.

NOTES TO CHAPTER 2

1. James Agee, *A Death in the Family* (New York: Bantam, 1981) All references to this novel are found in the text.
2. For an excellent discussion of religious models see Sallie McFague's, *Metaphorical Theology* (Philadelphia: Fortress, 1982).
3. Dwight MacDonald, *Against the American Grain* (New York: Random, 1962) 147.
4. Robert Coles, *Irony in the Mind's Life* (Charlottesville: U P of Virginia, 1974) 64.
5. James Agee, *The Collected Short Prose of James Agee*, Robert Fitzgerald, ed. (Dunwoody: Norman S. Berg, 1978) 141.
6. Robie Macauley and George Lanning, *Technique in Fiction* (New York: Harper, 1964) 100.
7. Coles, *Irony* 101.
8. For an excellent discussion of this idea, see Helene Cixous' *The Newly Born Woman*, Trans. Betsy Wing (Minnesota U P, 1986).

9. Woman becoming animal-like is not an unusual theme. See Margaret Atwood's *Surfacing*. Becoming bestial allows woman to evolve again, this time free of male expectations and restraints.

10. McFague, *Metaphorical* 142.

11. McFague, *Metaphorical* 142.

12. McFague, *Metaphorical* 182ff.

13. William James, *The Varieties of Religious Experience* (New York: Longmans, 1916) 507.

14. James, *Varieties* 489.

15. James, *Varieties* 31.

16. James, *Varieties* 486.

17. James, *Varieties* 512.

18. James, *Varieties* 175.

19. James, *Varieties* 187.

20. James, *Varieties* 196.

21. James, *Varieties* 176.

22. James, *Varieties* 51.

NOTES TO CHAPTER 3

1. The title of this chapter is taken from the general Confession of The Morning Prayer in *The Book of Common Prayer* (Edinburgh: D. Hunter Blair, 1827) 6.

2. Walker Percy, *The Message in the Bottle* (New York: Farrar, 1975) 111.

3. Percy, *Message* 111.

4. Percy, *Message* 111.

5. Walker Percy, *Love in the Ruins* (New York: Avon, 1971) All references to novel are noted in text.

6. Jean-Paul Sartre, *Nausea*, Trans. Bernard Frechtman (New York: Washington, 1966) 1.

7. Sartre, *Nausea* 8.

8. Sartre, *Nausea* 33.

9. Sartre, *Nausea* 54.

10. Sartre, *Nausea* 19.

11. Sartre, *Nausea* 156-7.

12. Sigmund Freud, *Civilization and Its Discontents*, Trans. James Strachey (New York: Norton, 1961) 65.

13. Freud, *Civilization* 77.

14. Percy, *Message* 24.

15. Herbert May and Bruce Metzger, *The New Oxford Annotated Bible with the Apocrypha*, Revised Standard Version (New York: Oxford U P, 1977) "Romans" 7.15b.

16. Soren Kierkegaard, *Repetition*, Trans. Walter Lowrie (New Jersey: Princeton U P, 1941) 200.

17. W. A. Mozart, *Don Giovanni*, libretto by Lorenzo Da Ponte, Trans. W. H. Auden and Chester Kallman (New York: Schirnier, 1961) All references to score and libretto are noted in text.

18. William Mann, *The Operas of Mozart* (London: Cassell, 1977) 460.

19. Mann, *Operas* 460.

20. W. L. Godshalk, "Walker Percy's Christian Vision," *Louisiana Studies* 13 (1974) 130.

21. Percy, *Message* 24.

22. Percy, *Message* 23.

23. Percy, *Message* 18.

24. Gerald Kennedy, "The Sundered Self and the Riven World: *Love in the Ruins*," in Panthea Reid Broughton, ed. *The Art of Walker Percy: Stratagems for Being* (Baton Rouge: Louisiana U P, 1979) 119.

25. Percy, *Message* 117.

26. Augustine, *The City of God*, Introduction, Vernon Burke; foreword, Etienne Gilson; Trans. Gerald Walsh, Demetrius Zema, Grace Monahan, Daniel Honan (New York: Image, 1958) 239.

27. Augustine, *City* 205.

28. Augustine, *City* 295.

29. Augustine, *City* 205.

30. Augustine, *City* 428.

31. Augustine, *City* 464.

32. Augustine, *City* 464.

33. Augustine, *City* 465.

34. Augustine, *City* 465.

35. Augustine, *City* 480.

36. Augustine, *City* 481.

37. Augustine, *City* 480.

38. Augustine, *City* 464.

39. Augustine, *City* 543.

40. Augustine, *City* 310.

NOTES TO CHAPTER 4

1. This language is from Paul Tillich's *The Courage to Be* (New Haven: Yale U P, 1952) and will be discussed more fully in the concluding comments of this chapter.

2. Dorethea Krook, *Elements of Tragedy* (New Haven: Yale U P, 1969) 43.

3. Robert Penn Warren, *A Place to Come To* (New York: Dell, 1977). All references to his novel are found in the text.

4. See particularly Cleanth Brooks' *The Hidden God* . (New Haven: Yale U P, 1963). Brooks argues that Warren uses, extensively, Christian language and ideology in his fiction.

5. Chester E. Eisinger, in *Robert Penn Warren: Critical Perspectives*, Neil Nakadate, ed. (Lexington: U Kentucky P, 1981). Eisinger's chapter explores, in part, Warren's disdain for such an optimistic view of human nature.

6. Robert Penn Warren, *Brother to Dragons* (New York: Random, 1953).

7. Warren, *Brother* 193.

8. Thomas L. Connelly, "Of Bookish Men and the Fugitives: A Conversation with Robert Penn Warren," an interview with Robert Penn Warren in *A Southern Renascence Man*, Walter B. Edgar, ed. (Baton Rouge: Louisiana State U P, 1984) 103.

9. Connelly, "Bookish Men," 103.

10. Tillich, *Courage* 9.

11. David Tracy, *Blessed Rage for Order* (New York: Seabury, 1978) 105. Tracy, in his discussion of limit-situations echoes Karl Jasper's concept of "boundary-situations," in *Philosophy*, vol. 2 (Chicago, U of Chicago P, 1970) 177-218.

12. Peter Stitt, "Robert Penn Warren: Life's Instancy and the Astrolabe Joy," *The Georgia Review* 34 (1980): 724.

13. Giles Gunn, *The Interpretation of Otherness* (New York: Oxford U P, 1979) 180.

14. See Wayne Booth's *The Rhetoric of Fiction* (Chicago: U of Chicago P, 1983), particularly his discussion on the author's voice in fiction, 169-211.

15. Wesley A. Kort, *Moral Fiber: Character and Belief in Recent Fiction* (Philadelphia: Fortress, 1982) 3.

16. For further exploration into the function and nature of tragedy see: Northrop Frye, *The Anatomy of Criticism: Four Essays* (Princeton: Princeton U P, 1957), Robert B. Heilman, *Tragedy and Melodrama* (U of Washington P, 1968), T. R. Henn, *The Harvest of Tragedy* (London: Methuen, 1956), Rene Girard, *Violence and the Sacred*, trans. Patrick Gregory (Baltimore: Johns Hopkins P, 1972), John D. Barbour, *Tragedy as a Critique of Virtue*, Chico: Scholars, 1984), Aristotle, *Poetics*, trans. Kenneth A. Telford (Indiana: Gateway, 1961), David H. Hesla, "Greek and Christian Tragedy," in *Art/Literature/Religion*, Robert Detweiler, ed. (Chico: Scholars, 1983): 71-87.

17. Tjebbe Westendrop, "*A Place to Come To*" in Richard Gray's *Robert Penn Warren: A Collection of Critical Essays*, (New Jersey: Prentice, 1980) 127.

18. Diane S. Bonds, "Vision and Being in *A Place to Come To*," *The Southern Review* 16 (1980): 816.

19. Richard Howard, "Dreadful Alternatives: A Note on Robert Penn Warren," *Georgia Review* 29 (1975): 38.

20. Nakadate, *Critical Perspectives* 12.

21. Marshall Walker, *Robert Penn Warren: A Vision Earned* (Glasgow: Barnes, 1979) 231.

22. Richard Gray, ed. *Robert Penn Warren: A Collection of Critical Essays* (New Jersey: Prentice, 1980) 2.

23. A critical reason for choosing Tillich to elucidate the religious dimensions of Warren's text is Tillich's favorable insights to the relation between Stoicism and twentieth century Protestant theology.

24. Paul Tillich, *Systematic Theology* (Chicago: U of Chicago P, 1957) vol. ii, 39.

25. Tillich, *Systematic* vol. ii, 37.

26. Tillich, *Systematic* vol. ii, 37.

27. Tillich, *Systematic* vol. ii, 38.

28. Tillich, *Courage* 32.

29. Tillich, *Courage* 42.
30. Tillich, *Courage* 43.
31. Tillich, *Courage* 47.
32. Tillich, *Courage* 49.
33. Tillich, *Courage* 50.
34. Tillich, *Courage* 51.
35. Tillich, *Courage* 52.

NOTES TO CHAPTER 5

1. Alasdair MacIntyre, *After Virtue* (Notre Dame: U of Notre Dame P, 1984) 216.
2. Jose Ortega y Gasset, *The Dehumanization of Art*, trans. Willard Trask (Princeton: Princeton U P, 1948) 13.
3. Wayne Booth, *The Rhetoric of Fiction* (Chicago: U of Chicago P, 1983) 43.
4. Booth, *Rhetoric* 60.
5. Barbara hardy, "An Approach Through Narrative," in *Towards a Poetic of Fiction*, Mark Spilka, ed. (Bloomington: Indiana U P, 1977) 31.
6. Hardy, "An Approach" 31.
7. Hardy, "An Approach" 31.
8. Hardy, "An Approach" 32.
9. Hardy, "An Approach" 35.
10. Hardy, "An Approach" 35.
11. Stephen Crites, "The Narrative Quality of Experience," *Journal of the American Academy of Religion* 39 (1971) 291.
12. MacIntyre, *Virtue* 206.
13. MacIntyre, *Virtue* 205.
14. MacIntyre, *Virtue* 206.
15. MacIntyre, *Virtue* 206.
16. MacIntyre, *Virtue* 208.
17. MacIntyre, *Virtue* 221.
18. MacIntyre, *Virtue* 208.
19. MacIntyre, *Virtue* 220.
20. MacIntyre, *Virtue* 215.
21. MacIntyre, *Virtue* 215.
22. MacIntyre, *Virtue* 215.
23. MacIntyre, *Virtue* 215-6.
24. MacIntyre, *Virtue* 216.
25. MacIntyre, *Virtue* 219.
26. MacIntyre, *Virtue* 219.
27. MacIntyre, *Virtue* 219.
28. Stanley Hauerwas, *A Community of Character* (Notre Dame: U of Notre Dame P, 1981) 132.
29. Stanley Hauerwas, *The Peaceable Kingdom* (Notre Dame: U of Notre Dame P, 1983) 21.
30. Hauerwas, *Community* 67.
31. Hauerwas, *Community* 132.

32. Stanley Hauerwas, *Character and the Christian Life* (San Antonio: Trinity U P, 1985) 18.

33. Hauerwas, *Character* 15.

34. Hauerwas, *Peaceable* 132.

35. Hauerwas, *Peaceable* 122.

36. Hauerwas, *Community* 136.

37. Hauerwas, *Community* 144.

38. Hauerwas, *Community* 144.

39. Hauerwas, *Community* 147.

40. Hauerwas, *Peaceable* 119.

41. Stanley Hauerwas, "Constancy and Forgiveness: The Novel as a School for Virtue," *Notre Dame English Journal* (1981) 43.

42. Hauerwas, "Constancy" 44.

43. Annie Dillard, *Living by Fiction* (New York: Harper, 1982) 183.

44. David Tracy, "Creativity in the Interpretation of Religion," *New Literary History* 15 (1984) 289.

45. Lionel Trilling, *Sincerety and Authenticity* (Cambridge: Harvard U P, 1972) 135.

46. Nathan Scott, "Reflections on the Present Crisis in Humanistic Studies," *The Virginia Quarterly* 62 (1986) 413.

47. Giles Gunn, "Moral Order in Modern Literature and Criticism: The Challenge of the 'new New Criticism'," in *Art/Literature/Religion: Life on the Borders* , Robert Detweiler, ed. (Chico: Scholars, 1983) 52.

48. Robert Scholes, *Textual Power* (New Haven: Yale U P, 1985) 87

49. Booth, *Rhetoric* 137.

50. Booth, *Rhetoric* 139.

51. Booth, *Rhetoric* 147.

52. MacIntyre, *Virtue* 211.

53. Booth, *Rhetoric* 385.

54. I am indebted to Paul Ricoeur for these phrases. See particularly *The Symbolism of Evil*, Trans. Emerson Buchanan (Boston: Beacon, 1967) and *Freud and Philosophy: An Essay on Interpretation*, Trans. Denis Savage (New Haven: Yale U P, 1970).

55. Scholes, *Textual* xi.

56. Tracy, "Creativity" 290.

57. Tracy, "Creativity" 296.

58. Tracy, "Creativity" 296.

59. Hans-Georg Gadamer, *Truth and Method* (New York: Seabury, 1975) 91ff, 274-305, and 325ff.

60. Tracy, "Creativity" 297.

61. Tracy, "Creativity" 300.

62. Tracy, "Creativity" 300.

63. Tracy, "Creativity" 302.

SELECTED BIBLIOGRAPHY

James Agee

Primary Sources

Agee, James. *Agee on Film: Reviews and Commentary.* New York: McDowell, 1958
---. *Agee on Film, Volume II: Five Film Scripts.* New York: McDowell, 1960.
---. *The Collected Poems of James Agee.* ed. Robert Fitzgerald. Boston: Houghton, 1968.
---. *The Collected Short Prose of James Agee.* ed. with a "Memoir" by Robert Fitzgerald. Boston: Houghton, 1968.
---. *A Death in the Family.* New York: McDowell, 1957.
---. *Four Early Stories by James Agee.* Collected by Elena Harap. West Branch: Cummington, 1964.
---. *The Letters of James Agee to Father Flye.* ed. James H. Flye. New York: George, 1962.
---. *The Letters of James Agee to Father Flye.* 2nd ed. Boston: Houghton, 1971.
---. *Let Us Now Praise Famous Men.* Forward, Walker Evans. Boston: Houghton, 1960.
---. *The Morning Watch.* Boston: Houghton, 1951.
---. *Permit Me Voyage.* New Haven: Yale U P, 1934.
---. *A Way of Seeing.* An Introduction to a book of photographs by Helen Levitt. New York: Viking, 1965.

Secondary Sources

Barson, Alfred T. *A Way of Seeing: A Critical Study of James Agee.* Amherst: U of Massachusetts P, 1972.
Bergreen, Laurence. *James Agee: A Life.* New York: Dutton, 1984.
Broughton, George and Panthea Reid. "Agee and Autonomy." *Southern Humanities Review* 4 (1970): 101-11.
Coles, Robert. *Irony in the Mind's Life: Essays on Novels by James Agee, Elizabeth Bowen, and George Eliot.* Charlotte: U P of Virginia, 1973.
---. "James Agee's 'Famous Men' Seen Again." *Harvard Advocate* 105 (1972): 42-6.

DaPont, Durant. "James Agee: The Quest for Identity." *Tennessee Studies in Literature*. 8 (1963): 25-37.

Doty, Mark. *Tell Me Who I Am: James Agee's Search for Self-hood*. Baton Rouge: Louisiana State U P, 1981.

Fiedler, Leslie. "Encounter with Death." Review of *A Death in the Family*. *New Republic* 9 (1957): 25-6.

Flye, Father James Harold. "An Article of Faith." *Harvard Advocate* 105 (1972): 15-7, 24.

Hayes, Richard. "James Agee: Rhetoric of Splendor." *Commonweal* 68 (1958): 591-92.

Holder, Alan. "Encounter in Alabama: Agee and the Tenant Farmers." *Virginia Quarterly Review* 42.

Kramer, Victor A. " Agee's Use of Regional Material in *A Death in the Family*." *Appalachian Journal* 1 (1972): 72-80.

---. *James Agee*. Boston: G. K., 1975.

Larson, Erling. *James Agee*. Minneapolis: U of Minnesota P, 1971.

Lawbaugh, William M. "'Remembrance of Things Past': An Analysis of James Agee's Prose Style." Diss. U of Missouri, Columbia, 1972.

Little, Michael Vincent. "Sacramental Realism in James Agee's Major Prose." Diss. U of Delaware, 1974.

MacDonald, Dwight. *Against the American Grain*. New York: Random, 1962.

---. "Death of a Poet." *The New Yorker* 33 (1957): 204-21.

---. "On Chaplin, Verdoux, and Agee." *Esquire* 63 (1965): 24-34.

Madden, David, ed. *Remembering James Agee*. Baton Rouge: Louisiana State U P, 1974.

Milner, Joseph O. "Autonomy and Communion in *A Death in the Family*." *Tennessee Studies in Literature* 21 (1976): 105-13.

Moreau, Genevieve. *The Restless Journey of James Agee* Trans. Miriam Kleiger. New York: William, 1977.

Ohlin, Peter. *Agee*. New York: Ivan, 1966.

Perry, Douglas Jr. "Thematic Counterpoint in *A Death in the Family* : The Function of the Six Extra Senses." *Novel* 5 (1971): 234-41.

Phillipson, J. S. "Character, Theme, and Symbol in *The Morning Watch*" *Western Humanities Review* 15 (1961): 359-67.

Rewak, William. "James Agee's *The Morning Watch*: Through Darkness to Light." *Texas Quarterly* 16 (1973): 21-37.

---. "The Shadow and the Butterfly: James Agee's Treatment of Death." Diss. U of Minnesota, 1970.

Roe, Michael M. "A Point of Focus in James Agee's *A Death in the Family*." *Tentieth Century Literature* 12 (1966-7): 149-53.

Samway, Patrick. "James Agee: A Family Man." *Thought* 47 (1971): 40-68.

Seib, Kenneth. *James Agee*. Pittsburgh: U of Pittsburgh P, 1968.

Shepherd, Allen. "'A Sort of Monstrous Grinding Beauty': Reflections on Character and Theme in James Agee's *A Death in he Family*." *Iowa English Year* (1969): 17-24.

Sosnoski, James J. "Craft and Intention In James Agee's *A Death in the Family*." *Journal of General Education* 20 (1968): 170-83

Ward, J. A. *"A Death in the Family* : the Importance of Wordlessness."
    Modern Fiction Studies 26 (1980-81): 597-611.
Whittier, Gayle. "Belief and Unbelief in *A Death in the Family."*
    Renascence 31 (1978): 172-92.

Walker Percy

Primary Sources

Percy, Walker. "The Coming Crisis in Psychiatry." *America* 96 (1957):
    391-3, 415-18.
---. *The Last Gentleman.* New York: Farrar, 1966.
---. *Lancelot.* New York: Farrar, 1977.
---. *Lost in the Cosmos.* New York: Farrar, 1983.
---. *Love in the Ruins.* New York: Farrar, 1971.
---. *The Message in the Bottle.* New York: Farrar, 1975.
---. "Mississippi: The Fallen Paradise." *Harper's* 230 (1956): 166-72.
---. "Modern Man on the Threshold." *America* 105 (1961): 612.
---. *The Moviegoer.* New York: Farrar, 1961.
---. *The Second Coming.* New York: Farrar, 1980.
---. "Stoicism in the South." *Commonweal* 64 (1956): 342-44.
---. *The Thanatos Syndrome.* New York: Farrar, 1987.

Secondary Sources

Allen, William Rodney. *Walker Percy: A Southern Wayfarer.* Jackson: U P
    of Mississippi, 1986.
Atkins, Anselm. "Walker Percy and Post-Christian Search." *Centennial
    Review* 12 (1968): 73-95.
Bigger, Charles P. "Logos and Epiphany: Walker Percy's Theology of
    Language." *Southern Review* 13 (1977): 196-206.
Blouin, Michael T. "The Novels of Walker Percy: An Attempt at
    Synthesis." *Xavier University Studies* 6 (1967): 29-42.
Bradbury, John M. "Absurd Insurrection: The Barth-Percy Affair." *South
    Atlanttic Quarterly* 3 (1969): 319-29.
Bradford, Melvin E. "Dr. Percy's Paradise Lost: Diagnostics in Louisiana."
    Sewanee Review 81 (1973): 839-44.
Bradley, Jared W. "Walker Percy and the Search for Wisdom." *Louisiana
    Studies* 4 (1973): 579-90.
Brinkmeyer, Robert H. "Percy's Bludgeon: Message and Narrative
    Strategy." *Southern Quarterly* 18 (1980): 80-90.
---. *Three Catholic Writers of the Modern South.* Jackson: U P of
    Mississippi, 1985.
Brooks, Cleanth. "Walker Percy and Modern Gnosticism." *Southern Review*
    13 (1977): 677-87.
Broughton, Panthea Reid. *The Art of Walker Percy: Stratagems for Being.*
    Baton Rouge: Louisiana State U P, 1979.

Brown, Ashley. "An Interview with Walker Percy." *Shenandoah* 3 (1967): 3-10.

Bunting, Charles T. "An Afternoon with Walker Percy." *Notes on Mississippi Writers* 2 (1971): 43-61.

Coles, Robert. *Walker Percy: An American Search.* Boston: Little, 1978.

Dowie, William. "Walker Percy: Sensualist-Thinker." *Novel* 6 (1972): 52-65.

Eubanks, Cecil L. "Walker Percy: Eschatology and the Politics of Grace." *Southern Quarterly* 18 (1980): 121-36.

Gaston, Paul L. "The Revelation of Walker Percy." *Colorado Quarterly* 4 (1972): 459-70.

Godshalk, William L. "Walker Percy's Christian Vision." *Louisiana Studies* 2 (1974): 130-141.

Hardy, John Edward. "Percy and Place: Some Beginnings and Endings." *Southern Quarterly* 18 (1980): 5-25.

Johnson, Mark. "The Search for Place in Walker Percy's Novels." *Southern Literary Journal* 3 (1975): 55-81.

Kazin, Alfred. "The Pilgrimage of Walker Percy." *Harper's* 242 (1971): 81-6.

Lawson, Lewis A. and Victor Kramer. *Conversations with Walker Percy.* Jackson: U P of Mississippi, 1985.

Lawson, Lewis A. "Walker Percy: the Physician as Novelist." *South Atlantic Bulletin* 2 (1972): 58-63.

---. "Walker Percy's Southern Stoic." *Southern Literary Journal* 1 (1970): 5-31.

LeClair, Thomas. "The Eschatological Vision of Walker Percy." *Renascence* 3 (1974): 115-22.

Lehan, Richard. *A Dangerous Crossing: French Literary Existentialism and the Modern American Novel.* Carbondale: Southern Illinois U P, 1973.

---. "The Way Back: Redemption in the Novels of Walker Percy." *Southern Review* 2 (1968): 306-19.

Luschei, Martin. *The Sovereign Wayfarer: Walker Percy's Diagnosis of the Malaise.* Baton Rouge: Louisiana State U P, 1972.

Pearson, Michael. "Art as Symbolic: Walker Percy's Aesthetic." *Southern Quarterly* 18 (1980): 55-64.

Poteat, Patricia Lewis. *Walker Percy and the Old Modern Age: Reflections on Language Arguement and the Telling of Stories.* Baton Rouge: Louisiana State U P, 1985.

Spivey, Ted R. *The Writer as Shaman.* Macon: Mercer U P, 1986.

Tanner, Tony. *The Reign of Wonder: Naivete and Reality in American Literature.* Cambridge: Cambridge U P, 1965.

Taylor, Jerome. *In Search of Self: Life, Death, and Walker Percy.* Cambridge: Cowley, 1986.

Telotte, J. P. "Walker Percy's Language of Creation." *Southern Quarterly* 16 (1978): 105-16.

---. "Walker Percy: A Pragmatic Approach." *Southern Studies* 18 (1979): 217-30.

Van Cleave, Jim. "Versions of Percy." *Southern Review* 3 (1970): 990-1010.

Vauthier, Simone. "Le Temps et Le Mort Dans The Moviegoer." *Recherches Anglaises et Americaines* 4 (1971): 98-115.
Zeugner, John F. "Walker Percy and Gabriel Marcel: The Castaway and the Wayfarer." *Mississippi Quarterly* 28 (1975): 21-53.

Robert Penn Warren

Primary Sources

Warren, Robert Penn. *All the King's Men* New York: Harcourt, 1946.
---. *At Heaven's Gate.* New York: Harcourt, 1943.
---. *Audubon: A Vision.* New York: Random, 1969.
---. *Band of Angels.* New York: Random, 1955.
---. *Being Here: Poetry 1977-80.* New York: Random, 1980.
---. *Blackberry Winter.* Cummington: Cummington, 1946.
---. *Brother to Dragons: A New Version.* New York: Random, 1979.
---. *The Cave.* New York: Random, 1959.
---. *Chief Joseph of the Nez Perce.* New York: Random, 1983.
---. *The Circus in the Attic and Other Stories.* New York: Harcourt, 1947.
---. *Eleven Poems on the Same Theme.* Norfolk: New Directions, 1942.
---. *Flood: A Romance of Our Time.* New York: Random, 1964.
---. *Incarnations: Poems 1966-1968.* New York: Random, 1968.
---. *Meet Me in the Green Glen.* New York: Random, 1971.
---. *New and Selected Poems, 1923-1985.* New York: Random, 1985.
---. *Night Rider.* Boston: Houghton, 1939.
---. *Now and Then: Poems 1976-1978.* New York: Random, 1978.
---. *Or Else--Poem/Poems 1968-74.* New York: Random, 1974.
---. *A Place to Come To.* New York: Random, 1977.
---. *Promises: Poems 1954-1956.* New York: Random, 1957.
---. *Rumor Verified: Poems 1979-1980.* New York: Random, 1981.
---. *Selected Poems.* New York: Harcourt, 1944.
---. *Wilderness: A Tale of the Civil War.* New York: Random, 1961.
---. *World Enough and Time.* New York: Random, 1950.

Secondary Sources

Bedient, Calvin. *In the Heart's Last Kingdom: Robert Penn Warren's Major Poetry* Cambridge: Harvard U P, 1984.
Bohner, Charles H. *Robert Penn Warren.* re. ed. Boston: Twayne, 1981.
Bonds, Diane S. "Vision and Being in *A Place to Come To.*" *The Southern Poetry.* Cambridge: Harvard U P, 1984.
Brooks, Cleanth. *The Hidden God: Studies in Hemingway, Faulkner, Yeats, Eliot, and Warren.* New Haven: Yale U P, 1963.
Casper, Leonard. *Robert Penn Warren: The Dark and Bloody Ground.* Seattle: U P of Washington, 1960.
Clark, William B., ed. *Critical Essays on Robert Penn Warren.* Boston: G. K.,1981.

Dooley, D. M. "The Persona Robert Penn Warren in Warren's *Brother to Dragons*. *Mississippi Quarterly* 25 (1971-2): 19-30.

Edgar, Walter B., ed. *A Southern Renascence Man.* Baton Rouge: Louisiana State U P, 1984.

Fiedler, Leslie A. "Three Notes on Robert Penn Warren," in *No! In Thunder: Essays on Myth and Literature.* Boston: Beacon, 1960. 119-133.

Gray, Richard, ed. *Robert Penn Warren.* Englewood Cliffs: Prentice, 1980.

Graziano, Frank, ed. *Homage to Robert Penn Warren.* Durango: Logbridge-Rhodes, 1981.

Grimshaw, James A. Jr., ed. *Robert Penn Warren's Brother to Dragons: A Discussion.* Baton Rouge: Louisiana State U P, 1983.

Guttenberg, Barnett. *Web of Being: The Novels of Robert Penn Warren.* Nashville: Vanderbilt U P, 1975.

Hicks, John. "Explorations of Value: Warren's Criticism." *South Atlantic Quarterly* 62 (1975): 37-41.

Justus, James H. *The Achievement of Robert Penn Warren* Baton Rouge: Louisiana State U P, 1981.

---. "The Politics of the Self-Created." *Sewanee Review* 82 (1974): 284-299.

Law, Richard. "*Brother to Dragons*: The Fact of Violence vs. the Possibility of Love." *American Literature* 49 (1978): 560-79.

Longley, John Lewis, Jr. ed. *Robert Penn Warren: A Collection of Critical Essays.* New York: U P, 1965.

Moore, L. Hugh. *Robert Penn Warren and History: "The Big Myth We Live."* The Hague: Mouton, 1970.

Nakadate, Neil, ed. *Robert Penn Warren.* Lexington: U P of Kentucky, 1981.

---. "Robert Penn Warren and the Confessional Novel." *Genre* 2 (1969): 326-40.

---. "Voices of Community: The Function of Colloquy in Robert Penn Warren's *Brother to Dragons*." *Tennessee Studies in Literature* 21 (1976): 114-24.

Rotella, Guy. "'One Flesh': Robert Penn Warren's I." *Renascence* 31 (1978): 25-42.

Shepherd, Allen. "Character and Theme in Warren's *Meet Me in the Green Glen*." *Greyfriar* 13 (1972): 34-41.

Snipes, Katherine. *Robert Penn Warren.* New York: Ungar, 1983.

Stitt, Peter. "Robert Penn Warren: Life's Instancy and the Astrolabe Joy." *The Georgia Review* 34 (1980): 711-31.

---. "Robert Penn Warren, the Poet." *Southern Review* 12 (1976): 261-76.

Strandberg, Victor H. *A Colder Fire: The Poetry of Robert Penn Warren.* Lexington: U of Kentucky P, 1965.

---. "Robert Penn Warren, the Poet." *Southern Review* 12 (1976): 261-76.

Walker, Marshall. "Making Dreams Work: The Achievement of Robert Penn Warren." *London Magazine* 15 (1975-6): 33-46.

Walker, Marshall. *Robert Penn Warren: A Vision Earned.* New York: Barnes, 1979.

Watkins, Floyd C. and John T. Heirs, eds. *Robert Penn Warren Talking: Interviews, 1950-1978*. New York: Random, 1980.

General Critical and Theoretical Studies

Abrams, M. H. *The Mirror and the Lamp: Romantic Theory and the Critical Tradition*. New York: Norton, 1958.
Auerbach, Erich. *Mimesis: The Representation of Reality in Western Literature*. Trans. Willard Trask. Princeton: Princeton U P, 1953.
Augustine. *The City of God*. Trans. Vernon J. Bourke. New York: Image,1958.
---. *Confessions*. Trans. R. S. Pine-Coffin. London: Penguin, 1961.
Barbour, John D. *Tragedy as a Critique of Virtue: The Novel and Ethical Reflection*. Chico: Scholars, 1984.
Bleicher, Josef. *Contemporary Hermeneutics: Hermeneutics as Method, Philosophy and Critique*. London: Routledge, 1983.
Booth, Wayne C. *The Rhetoric of Fiction* 2nd ed. Chicago: U of Chicago P,1983.
Brake, Mike, ed. *Human Sexual Relations: Towards a Redefinition of Sexual Politics*. New York: Pantheon, 1982.
Brockelman, Paul. *Time and Self: Phenomenological Explorations*. New York: Crossroad, 1985.
Brooks, Peter. *Reading for the Plot: Design and Intention in Narration*. New York: Vintage, 1984.
Chatman, Seymour. *Story and Discourse: Narrative Structure in Fiction and Film*. Ithaca: Cornell U P, 1978.
Crites, Stephen. "The Narrative Quality of Experience." *Journal of the American Academy of Religion* (1971): 291-311.
Daiches, David. *God and the Poets*. Oxford: Clarendon, 1985.
Detweiler, Robert, ed. *Art/Literature/Religion: Life on the Borders*. Chico: Scholars, 1983.
Detweiler, Robert and Glenn Meeters, eds. *Faith and Fiction:The Modern Short Story*. Grand Rapids: Eerdmans, 1979.
Detweiler, Robert, ed. *Reader Response Approaches to Biblical and Secular Texts*. Decatur: Scholars, 1985.
De Unamuno, Miguel. *Tragic Sense of Life*. Trans. J. E. Crawford Flitch. New York: Dover, 1954.
Dillard, Annie. *Living By Fiction*. New York: Harper, 1982.
Edwards, Michael. *Towards A Christian Poetics*. Grand Rapids: Eerdmans,1984.
Eliade, Mircea. *The Sacred and the Profane*. Trans. Willard R. Trask. New York: Harper, 1961.
Eliot, T. S. *Selected Essays*. New York: Harcourt, 1964.
Frankl, Viktor E. *Psychotherapy and Existentialism*. New York: Touchstone, 1967.
Freud, Sigmund. *Beyond the Pleasure Principle*. trans. James Strachey. New York: Norton, 1961.
---. *Civilization and Its Discontents*. trans. James Strachey. New York: Norton, 1961.

---. *The Ego and the Id*. trans. Joan Riviere. Ed. James Strachey. New York: Norton, 1950.

---. *Totem and Taboo*. trans. James Strachey. New York: Norton, 1950.

Frye, Northrop. *Anatomy of Criticism: Four Essays*. Princeton: Princeton U P, 1957.

Gadamer, Hans-Georg. *Truth and Method*. New York: Seabury, 1975.

Gardner, John. *The Art of Fiction*. New York: Vintage, 1985.

Garvin, Harry R. *Literature, Arts, and Religion*. Lewisburg: Buckness U P, 1982.

Gasset, Ortega Y. *The Dehumanization of Art*. Trans. Willard Trask. Princeton: Princeton U P, 1948.

Genette, Girard. *Narrative Discourse*. Trans. Jane E. Lewin. Ithaca: Cornell U P, 1985.

Girard, Rene. *Deceit, Desire, and the Novel*. Trans. Yvonne Freccero. Baltimore: Johns Hopkins U P, 1965.

---. *Violence and the Sacred*. trans. Patrick Gregory. Baltimore: Johns Hopkins U P, 1972.

Graff, Gerald. *Literature Against Itself*. Chicago: U of Chicago P, 1979.

Gunn, Giles. *The Interpretation of Otherness*. New York: Oxford, 1979.

Hauerwas, Stanley. *Character and the Christian Life*. San Antonio: Trinity U P, 1985.

---. *A Community of Character*. Notre Dame: U of Notre Dame P, 1986.

---. "Constancy and Forgiveness: The Novel as a School for Virtue." *Notre Dame English Journal* (1981) 23-34.

---. *The Peaceable Kingdom*. Notre Dame: U of Notre Dame P, 1983.

Heilman, Robert B. *Tragedy and Melodrama*. Seattle: U of Washington P, 1968.

Heller, Erich. *The Artist's Journey into the Interior and Other Essays*. New York: Harcourt, 1965.

Henn, T. R. *The Harvest of Tragedy*. London: Methuen, 1956.

Hesla, David H. "Religion and Literature: The Second Stage." *Journal of Theology* 46 (1978): 181-192.

Higbie, Robert. *Character and Structure in the English Novel*. Gainesville: U of Florida P, 1984.

Iser, Wolfgang. *The Act of Reading: A Theory of Aesthetic Response*. Baltimore: Johns Hopkins U P, 1981.

James, Henry. *The Art of Fiction*. New York, 1948.

James, William. *The Varieties of Religious Experience* London: Longmans, 1916.

Jefferson, Douglas and Graham Martin, eds. *The Uses of Fiction*. Milton Keynes: Open U P, 1982.

Kahler, Erich. *The Inward Turn of Narrative*. trans. Richard and Clara Winston. Princeton: Princeton U P, 1973.

Kermode, Frank. *The Genesis of Secrecy*. Cambridge: Harvard U P, 1979.

---. *The Sense of an Ending*. London: Oxford U P, 1966.

Kierkegaard, Soren. *Christian Discourses*. Trans. Walter Lowrie. Princeton: Princeton U P, 1974.

---. *Fear and Trembling and the Sickness Unto Death*. Trans. Walter Lowrie. Princeton: Princeton U P, 1954.

---. *Repetition*. Trans. Walter Lowrie. Princeton: Princeton U P, 1941.

Klemm, David E. *The Interpretation of the Texts*. Atlanta: Scholars, 1986. Vol. 1 of *Hermeutical Inquiry*. 2 vols.

Konigsberg, Ira. *Narrative Technique in the English Novel* Connecticut: Archon, 1985.

Kort, Wesley. *Narrative Elements and Religious Meaning*. Philadelphia: Fortress, 1975.

---. Moral Fiber: *Character and Belief in Recent American Fiction*. Philadelphia: Fortress, 1982.

Krook, Dorethea. *Elements of Tragedy*. New Haven: Yale U P, 1969.

Lasch, Christopher. *The Culture of Narcissism*. New York: Warner, 1979.

Shirley, Robin Letwin. *The Gentleman in Trollope: Individuality and Moral Conduct*. Cambridge: Harvard U P, 1982.

Lubbock, Percy. *The Craft of Fiction*. New York: Viking, 1960.

Macauley, Robie and George Lanning. *Technique in Fiction*. New York: Harper, 1964.

MacIntyre, Alasdair. *After Virtue*. 2nd ed. Notre Dame: U of Notre Dame P, 1984.

Mallard, William. *The Reflection of Theology in Literature: A Case Study in Theology and Culture*. San Antonio: Trinity U P, 1977.

May, Herbert G. and Bruce M. Metzger. *The New Oxford Annotated Bible With The Apocrypha*, Revised Standard Version. New York: Oxford U P, 1977.

McFague, Sallie. *Metaphorical Theology*. Philadelphia: Fortress, 1982.

Nietzsche, Friedrich. *The Birth of Tragedy and The Case of Wagner*. Trans. Walter Kaufmann. New York: Vintage, 1967.

O'Connor, Flannery. *Mystery and Manners*. New York: Farrar, 1969.

O'Connor, William Van. *An Age of Criticism: 1900-1950*. Minneapolis: Gateway, 1966.

Otto, Rudolf. *The Idea of the Holy*. London: Oxford U P, 1923.

Putzell-Korab, Sara and Robert Detweiler, eds. *The Crisis in the Humanities: Interdisciplinary Responses*. Potomac: Studia Humanitatis, 1983.

Ransom, John Crowe. *Beating the Bushes: Selected Essays 1941- 1970*. New York: New Directions, 1972.

---. *The World's Body*. Baton Rouge: Louisiana State U P, 1968.

Rauschenbusch, Walter. *A Theology for the Social Gospel* Nashville: Abingdon, 1978.

Ricoeur, Paul. *The Conflict of Interpretations*. Evanston: Northwestern U P, 1974.

---. *Time and Narrative*. vol. 2. Trans. Kathleen McLoughlin and David Pellaues. Chicago: U of Chicago P, 1985. 2 vols.

Sartre, Jean-Paul. *Existentialism and Human Emotions*. New York: Wisdom, 1957.

---. *Nausea*. Trans. Lloyd Alexander. New York: New Directions, 1964.

Scholes, Robert, ed. *Approaches to the Novel*. San Francisco: Chandler, 1961.

---. *Structuralism in Literature: An Introduction*. New Haven: Yale U P, 1974.

---. *Textual Power*. New Haven: Yale U P, 1985.

Scott, Nathan. "Reflections on the Present Crisis in Humanistic Studies." *The Virginia Quarterly Review* 62 (1986): 402-21.

Scott, Wilbur S. *Five Approaches of Literary Criticism*. London: Collier, 1962.

Shlomith,Rimmon-Kenan*Narrative Fiction: Contemporary Poetics*. New York: Methuen, 1983.

Spilka, Mark, ed. *Towards a Poetics of Fiction*. Bloomington: Indiana U P, 1977.

Steiner, George. *In Bluebeard's Castle: Some Notes Towards the Redefinition of Culture*. New Haven: Yale U P, 1971.

Telford, Kenneth. *Aristotle's Poetics: Translation and Analysis*. South Bend: Gateway, 1961.

Thompson, John B., ed. and Trans. *Paul Ricoeur: Hermeneutics and the Human Sciences*. London: Cambridge U P, 1982.

Todorov, Tzvetan. *The Poetics of Prose*. trans. Richard Howard. Foreword by Jonathan Cueller. New York: Cornell U P, 1977.

Tillich, Paul. *The Courage to Be*. New Haven: Yale U P, 1952.

---. *Systematic Theology*. vol. 1. Chicago: U of Chicago P, 1951. 3 vols.

---. *Systematic Theology*. vol. 2. Chicago: U of Chicago P, 1957. 3 vols.

---. *Systematic Theology*. vol. 3. Chicago: U of Chicago P, 1963. 3 vols.

---. *Theology of Culture*. London: Oxford U P, 1980.

Tracy, David. *The Analogical Imagination: Christian Theology and the Culture of Pluralism*. New York: Crossroad, 1981.

---. *Blessed Rage for Order: The New Pluralism in Theology*. New York: Seabury, 1978.

---. "Creativity in the Interpretation of Religion." *New Literary History* 15 (1984): 289-309.

---. *Plurality and Ambiguity: Hermeneutics, Religion, Hope* San Francisco: Harper, 1987.

Trilling, Lionel. *Sincerity and Authenticity*. Cambridge: Harvard U P, 1972.

Wellek, Rene, and Austin Warren. *Theory of Literature*. New York: Harcourt, 1956.

Welty, Eudora. *The Eye of the Story*. New York: Vintage, 1979.

Wiggins, James, ed. *Religion as Story*. New York: Harper, 1975.

Wimsatt, William K. Jr., and Cleanth Brooks. *Literary Criticism: A Short History*. New York: Knopf, 1964.